ANURADHA KAPOOR

LEAPS AND BOUNDS

BlueRose ONE
Stories Matter
NewDelhi • London

BLUEROSE PUBLISHERS
India | U.K.

Copyright © Anuradha Kapoor 2024

All rights reserved by author. No part of this publication may be reproduced, stored in a retrieval system or transmitted in any form or by any means, electronic, mechanical, photocopying, recording or otherwise, without the prior permission of the author. Although every precaution has been taken to verify the accuracy of the information contained herein, the publisher assumes no responsibility for any errors or omissions. No liability is assumed for damages that may result from the use of information contained within.

BlueRose Publishers takes no responsibility for any damages, losses, or liabilities that may arise from the use or misuse of the information, products, or services provided in this publication.

For permissions requests or inquiries regarding this publication, please contact:

BLUEROSE PUBLISHERS
www.BlueRoseONE.com
info@bluerosepublishers.com
+91 8882 898 898
+4407342408967

ISBN: 978-93-6783-669-9

Cover design: Shivam
Typesetting: Namrata Saini

First Edition: December 2024

Dedication

To my beloved father,
Mr. Vinod Kumar Suri,

Your unwavering support, guidance, and love have been the driving force behind my endeavors. This book is a testament to the values you instilled in me. I hope it makes you proud.

Foreword

I recommend "Leaps and Bounds" to every woman out there—these stories are us! They're relatable and resonate with our own journeys. Every woman has faced challenges that echo our lives, from battling self-doubt to juggling responsibilities and daring to dream big.

These 24 incredible women in the book turn setbacks into setups for something amazing, proving that life isn't always about playing it safe. Sometimes, you have just got to leap - and let's be honest, we do that all the time! This book is a joyful rollercoaster filled with inspiration, laughter, and that little voice saying, "I can totally do this!"

Dive into their quirky wisdom and heartwarming triumphs, and remember- the path to passion is paved with stumbles—and that's perfectly okay!

Get ready to leap into your own adventure and I am sure you are going to enjoy the ride!

-Shibani Sethi

Acknowledgments

I am deeply grateful to those who have supported me throughout this journey.

To my husband, Rajiv Kapoor, thank you for being my rock, providing encouragement, and believing in me.

To my children, Viraj and Kamakshi, your love has been invaluable. May this book inspire you to chase your dreams.

To my mother, Poonam Suri, your selflessness and strength have been a constant source of inspiration.

To my family, friends, and well-wishers, your unwavering support and enthusiasm have meant the world to me.

Thank you to everyone who has contributed to making "LEAPS AND BOUNDS" a reality.

Preface

In the vibrant tapestry of India, there are countless women who have dared to dream, defied conventions, and achieved the extraordinary. Their stories, often unsung, are testaments to the power of resilience, determination, and courage.

"LEAPS AND BOUNDS" is a celebration of these inspiring women, who have shattered glass ceilings, challenged societal norms, and paved the way for others to follow. This anthology brings together stories of entrepreneurs, artists, leaders, and change-makers from diverse backgrounds and regions, united by their unwavering spirit and unrelenting passion.

Through these pages, I invite you to meet the women who are redefining what's possible. Their journeys, marked by triumphs and setbacks, offer valuable lessons in perseverance, innovation, and self-discovery.

This book is more than a collection of stories – it's a testament to the transformative potential of women's empowerment. It's a reminder that every leap, every bound, and every courageous step forward has the power to inspire, educate, and uplift.

As you turn these pages, I hope you'll find inspiration in the struggles and successes of these remarkable women. May their stories ignite a fire within you, fueling your own passions, dreams, and aspirations.

Join me on this journey, as we honor the women who are shaping India's future, one leap at a time.

- Anuradha

Empowered Strides

Across India's diverse lands,
Women rise, with courageous hands.
Breaking barriers, shattering glass,
Their stories woven, forever to last.

With every leap, they pave the way,
For others to follow, come what may.
Their bounds, a testament to might,
Inspiring generations, shining bright.

From villages to cities, they stride,
With resilience, determination inside.
Against odds, they stand tall and strong,
Their voices echoing, righting wrong.

From entrepreneurs to artists bold,
Leaders, change-makers, young and old.
Their journeys, a tapestry so fine,
Interwoven with courage, heart, and mind.

LEAPS AND BOUNDS, their stories told,
A tribute to women, brave and bold.
May their struggles, triumphs, and strife,
Ignite the fire, that fuels new life.

May this anthology be a guiding light,
That shines upon, the darkest night.
May every reader, find inspiration true,
In the leaps and bounds, these women pursue.

Contents

1. Harmony in Simplicity 1
   Usha Uthup
2. Perseverance is thy name!! 7
   Tisca Chopra
3. Threads of Resilience 12
   Shamlu Dudeja
4. Draping Seamless Elegance 19
   Dolly Jain
5. Against The Tide 25
   Bula Choudhary
6. Footprints of Impact 31
   Mukta Nain
7. Skybound Dreams 38
   Archana Kapoor
8. Achieve Your Dream, Change Your Destiny 44
   Pinky Kapoor
9. Life is a miracle 50
   Nehha Fatehpuria
10. Beauty At Her Fingertips 56
    Bridgette Jones
11. Closing deals in heels 62
    Mamta Binani
12. A Warrior Princess 67
    Shobhika Kalra

13. Life Is Art, Live Yours in Colour.............................. 72
    Surabhi Agarwal

14. Harmony of Empowerment......................... 79
    Kavita Agarwal

15. Inspiring Confidence in Others 85
    Shashi Jain

16. From Kolkata's Hues to ELEGANCE 91
    Sharda Kasera

17. Coloring Innermost Cores.. 97
    Madhuri Mantri

18. Bold Beginnings.. 102
    Sarla Newatia

19. Lead, Inspire, Transform... 109
    Prerna Kothari Fomra

20. Feast of Ambition 114
    Vanita Bajoria

21. Lights, Camera, Action... 120
    Saroj Tivary

22. Navigating Love, Leadership, and the Leap 126
    Soma Roy

23. Culinary Canvas 132
    Sonal Athwani

24. Journey of Rediscovery 137
    Anuradha Kapoor

1

Harmony in Simplicity

Usha Uthup

"In the hallowed notes of time, a legendary singer crafts a symphony of emotions, their voice echoing through the ages, an immortal melody that resonates in the hearts of all who listen"

In the quaint town of Mumbai, a young girl reveled in the joy of a harmonious childhood. Growing up in a happy middle class family, her early years were filled with the vibrant colors of Indian culture. The young girls innate curiosity led her to explore the diverse sounds around her, creating a foundation for her future musical journey. With a heart full of contentment and a radiant smile that mirrored the warmth of her upbringing, little did she know that the rhythmic lullabies and lively folk tunes of her youth would evolve into the soul-stirring melodies that would later captivate audiences around the world. The carefree laughter of her childhood echoed through the corridors of her memory, laying the groundwork for the charismatic and innovative artist she would become.

Born in the bustling city of Mumbai in 1947, her early life seemed unlikely to forecast the musical powerhouse she would become. Growing up, Usha's exposure to diverse genres shaped her passion for singing from an early age. Her roots were firmly planted in a humble upbringing, with her father serving in the police force. Being the fifth among six siblings, she cherished the simplicity of their lifestyle. Usha often reflects on the contrast between the focused determination of her middle-class background and the open-ended mindset of today's youth. She believes that having too many options can hinder the courage needed to take a leap in life, emphasizing the importance of focus. Growing up, their modest means reflected in simple necessities, like Bata shoes and limited school uniforms. Despite these constraints, Usha's family found happiness in what they had, instilling in her a sense of contentment that transcends material possessions. She proudly carries this feeling of fulfillment into her present, unapologetically embracing her unique style. Usha's love for routine, unlike the modern preference for constant novelty, kept her grounded. Her childhood pleasures, from playing traditional games to enjoying radio shows, laid the foundation for her later success.

It was in school that a teacher's critique of her voice turned into a catalyst for transformation. Usha's ability to turn limitations into strengths became a guiding principle, emphasizing the importance of adapting aspirations to one's capabilities. The middle-class ethos, combined with her appreciation for India's rich linguistic diversity, forms the essence of Usha Uthup's remarkable journey. Her upbringing not only shaped her values but also instilled in her a sense of focus and gratitude. Usha's educational journey in a convent school exposed her to a multilingual environment, fostering her love for languages and reinforcing her pride in India's diverse cultural tapestry.

The turning point in Usha's life came during her school days when a teacher, recognizing her unique voice, provided a pivotal moment of encouragement. Instead of viewing her voice as a limitation, Usha embraced its distinctiveness, setting the stage for her future success. This resilience and ability to make the most of what she had became a mantra for her, urging others to cut their coat according to the material they possessed.

Her journey took a significant turn when she moved to Kolkata in the 1960s. The city's vibrant cultural scene became the backdrop for Usha's musical odyssey. Stepping into the world of nightclubs, she began belting out tunes that would soon capture the hearts of listeners. Usha's unique voice, blending traditional Indian melodies with Western influences, set her apart in the competitive scenario.

Her foray into the music scene gained momentum through her association with Radio Ceylon, a popular radio station of that era. This exposure not only widened her audience but also became a stepping stone to her remarkable journey. Trincas, a famed nightclub in Kolkata, played a crucial role in shaping her career. It was here that Usha's electrifying performances captured the attention of music enthusiasts and catapulted her to stardom.

Her gratitude for Radio Ceylon and Trincas is profound, as she attributes much of her success to these platforms. Radio Ceylon provided her with a broader platform to showcase her talent, reaching audiences beyond geographical boundaries. Trincas, on the other hand, became a crucial stage where her unique fusion of Indian and Western music found its roots. These experiences not only defined her musical style but also solidified her reputation as a groundbreaking artist.

In an era dominated by established playback singers, Usha Uthup dared to be different. She fearlessly sang in multiple languages, effortlessly switching between Hindi, Tamil, Bengali, and more. This multilingual prowess not only showcased her versatility but also endeared her to audiences across the country.

Usha rose to national fame with chart-topping hits like the iconic "Ramba Ho" and "Darling." The former, from the Bollywood movie "Armaan," not only became a cultural phenomenon but also solidified Usha's status as a musical trailblazer. Her fusion of Indian classical elements with Western beats became her signature style, earning her accolades and a devoted fan base.

Beyond her musical achievements, Usha Uthup is equally known for her vibrant and unconventional fashion sense. The singer's penchant for bold and colorful sarees and signature 'bindis' became as much a part of her identity as her soul-stirring voice. She became an icon for celebrating cultural diversity and breaking the norms of the traditionally conservative music industry.

Usha's journey transcended national boundaries. Her international performances brought Indian music to global stages, earning her recognition and respect worldwide. From New York to Tokyo, Usha Uthup's concerts showcased the universal appeal of her music and the power of cultural exchange.

As the years rolled on, Usha continued to reinvent herself, collaborating with new artists and experimenting with different genres. Her timeless appeal and energetic stage presence made her a symbol of enduring passion for music. Apart from several awards and accolades to her credit, she was recently awarded the very prestigious Padma Bhushan award for her contribution to music and Indian culture.

In the tapestry of Usha Uthup's life, the threads of resilience, innovation, and cultural celebration are woven together. Her story is not just about music; it's a narrative of breaking barriers, embracing diversity, and leaving an indelible mark on the world stage. Usha Uthup remains an inspiration for aspiring musicians and a living testament to the transformative power of music across borders.

Usha Uthup's journey from a middle-class upbringing to the international stage is a testament to the power of embracing one's roots, turning limitations into strengths, and finding success in unexpected places. Her story serves as an inspiration, illustrating that focus, resilience, and gratitude can pave the way for extraordinary achievements.

In the realm of melodies, where voices intertwine,
A legend emerges, a star that does shine.
Usha Uthup, a name etched in song,
Her voice, a river, flowing strong.
From Kolkata's heart to the world's embrace,
A singer whose passion leaves no trace.
Saree-clad and with a vibrant smile,
Her tunes dance, crossing every mile.
In the golden era of music's grace,
Usha's voice found its sacred space.
A soulful ballad or a rhythmic beat,
Her vocal prowess, a musical feat.
From "Hare Rama Hare Krishna" to "Ramba Ho,"
Her songs, like a river, constantly flow.
A fusion of cultures in each note she sings,
Usha Uthup, where diversity springs.
With a bindi on her forehead, a symbol so true,
She breaks through boundaries, creating anew.
An icon of strength, in music's attire,
Usha's legacy, a burning fire.
A voice that resonates through time,
In every lyric, her spirit does climb.
Usha Uthup, a legend so grand,
Her songs, forever, etched in the sand.

2

Perseverance is thy name!!

Tisca Chopra

"In the spotlight of dreams, a female actor graces the stage, embodying strength, grace, and the power to breathe life into every role she embraces"

The snow continued falling. The wind stirred among the trees that covered the hillsides and every shrub, every leaf and twig, bore it's feathery, white load. Amidst the pristine surroundings, the soft sound of a girl's fun-loving giggle could be heard. She danced and pranced around the house happily. Happy because these surroundings made her so and also because this was her home. Away from the chaotic life of the city, this little girl's home lay between the snow-capped mountains. The sweet giggle belonged to a little girl who had just sat down in a corner of the house, to read her favourite story book. Books delighted her the most and she spent hours reading them and when her imagination wanted to run freely, she would get busy sketching her dreams on the snowy canvas outside.

Tisca was born and brought up in Kasauli, Himachal Pradesh, into a family of educationists. Her parents were teachers at The Lawrence School Sanawar, nestled in nature's verdant embrace. After a few years, Tisca and her parents shifted base to Kabul Afghanistan, as her father was posted there as the Principal of India International School. Because of her stint at the International School, she made friends with the expats kids studying there and was therefore lucky to be friendly to children coming from all across the globe, including those from Afghanistan as well.

At present, Tisca Chopra is a popular name from the Indian film industry who has successfully pursued direction, production, scriptwriting, acting and lots more. Tisca - a concoction of beauty and brains, elucidated her multitasking persona phenomenally. Even though she did taste her share of setbacks and failures, she took it all in her stride by wonderfully manifesting her dreams and she soon set her charm over Indian cinema with her pleasing personality, impeccable beauty and sharp mind and is slowly reaching the pinnacle of success she had set out for.

Tisca graduated from Apeejay School Noida where her father was the principal and later studied English

Literature at Hindu College, University of Delhi. During her college days, she started working actively with amateur theatre but did not undergo any professional training to become an actor. Her first Bollywood film was a flop because of the same reason which Tisca realized later and decided to train in acting under the tutelage of some renowned theatre personalities.

This was the major leap in Tisca's life when she did not let the failure of her first film dishearten her and instead she took the failure as a challenge, enrolled herself into an acting course and waited for her dreams to turn into reality. She firmly believes that hardwork always pays off and with her dedication and versatility as an actor, Tisca is the first choice of many directors and has been offered many projects for cinema, television and OTT platforms.

Like many others, Tisca was also an outsider when she decided to pursue acting as a career and similar to all aspiring actors who have godfathers in the film industry, even her dream of working in Bollywood was next to attaining nirvana. In a country of more than 1.2 billion people, making space for yourself in the film industry is extremely tough, if not impossible. Thousands land up in Mumbai everyday to pursue their dreams and thousands return without realizing them but then there are tough ones like Tisca who deftly carve their way through.

On and off the screen, Tisca epitomizes elegance, sophistication and taste. Her role in 'Taare Zameen Par' brought her immense applause along with several national and international awards, where she played the role of a mother. After tasting success in films, she went on to author two books namely 'Acting smart' and 'What's up with me'. Apart from penning down her thoughts and being a regular on stage and cinema, she is also a favourite with advertisers. Tisca owns a YouTube channel 'Tisca's table' where she indulges in candid chats with various individuals.

Tisca ventured into production with short film 'Chutney' that has garnered over 135 million views on YouTube and several million views on OTT platforms as well. She now has her heart and mind set on pursuing film direction.

Bollywood, the 'dreamland' where we all, at some point in our lives have aspired to be or atleast fantasized about it, is not an easy thing to achieve. It is not easy to create a name for yourself in an industry where thousands of immensely talented individuals try their luck everyday. While it is comparatively easy to gain entry in Bollywood for star kids, it can be really difficult if you do not have any inside connection. However, there are people like Tisca Chopra who with their hardwork, perseverance and resilience break all constraints and stereotypes and achieve their goals. Women like her pave a path for other women to take the biggest leap in their life and follow their passion.

Women are known to have better intuition, patience, emotional focus, compassion and more. The list is endless but stories of women such as Tisca Chopra inspire us to channel our inner queen warrior and take that leap to tap into our power that will eventually lead us to leave an indelible mark on people close to us and the society at large.

Upon the stage where dreams take flight,
An actor graces, bathed in spotlight.
With scripts as her canvas, emotions unfurl,
She breathes life into characters, a mesmerizing swirl.
In the limelight's glow, she takes her cue,
A thespian's journey, where tales accrue.
From comedic highs to dramatic lows,
She transforms scripts into riveting shows.
With every gesture, a story's refrain,
An actor captivates, leaving an indelible stain.
In the theatre's hush or on the silver screen,
She embodies narratives, both bold and serene.
Through makeup's touch and costumes adorned,
She steps into roles, her passion adorned.
In the makeup chair, a chameleon's grace,
She metamorphoses, embracing each face.
In the world of make-believe, where stories entwine,
An actor's craft, a captivating design.
A conduit of emotions, in each scene's trance,
She dances through roles, in a rhythmic dance.
From curtain calls to the closing scene,
An actor breathes life into the unseen.
In the applause that echoes, a tale unfolds,
An actor's journey, where magic holds.

3

Threads of Resilience

Shamlu Dudeja

"Embrace change, unleash your passions, and let resilience be the thread that weaves your unique journey through the fabric of life"

In the heart of Karachi, the bustling city of pre-partition India, a young girl witnessed the unfolding tapestry of history. She navigated the complex dynamics of the partition era, a time marked by social upheaval and political turmoil. Her formative years unfolded amidst the echoes of change, where the intricate threads of society were being rewoven. Little did this young observer realize that her journey, intricately woven with the threads of her experiences, would sew through the fabric of time, leaving an indelible mark on the cultural and artistic landscape of India.

Born in pre-partition era in 1938, Shamlu Dudeja's early years were marked by the challenges of those times. Growing up amidst historical events, she attended a Sindhi medium school where her grasp of the English language was limited. The growing tensions between India and Pakistan, coupled with her father's concern for the family's safety during riots, prompted a significant decision to shift to India. Their journey involved a ship to Mumbai with minimal belongings, where they sought refuge with her maternal uncle, a film maker. Shamlu's father, a mathematics professor, took on the challenge of finding employment in Delhi, leading to the family's eventual relocation. Despite the initial language barrier, Shamlu's academic journey unfolded at Lady Irwin school, followed by graduation at Miranda House. This phase laid the foundation for her later pursuits in both mathematics and the world of Kantha embroidery.

Following her academic journey, Shamlu Dudeja's life took a turn when she married a tea merchant from Kolkata. The turning point, however, occurred when she encountered Kantha artisans at a handicrafts fair in Kolkata. Impressed by their craftsmanship, she entrusted them with white silk sarees to embellish with Kantha embroidery. When the artisans didn't return promptly, Shamlu, accompanied by her daughter, ventured to Shantiniketan in search of them. This journey marked the beginning of a profound connection with Kantha embroidery, as they discovered skilled women creating masterpieces in the form of sarees, dupattas, and more. What began as a personal fascination turned into a transformative initiative as Shamlu started taking orders, passing them on to the Kantha artisans in villages, and using the profits to empower them. This marked the inception of her mission to revive and sustain the indigenous art form of Bengal, ultimately making Kantha a source of livelihood for rural women. Shamlu Dudeja's journey from a simple rendezvous to empowering local artisans became a testament to her dedication and resilience in fostering creativity and financial independence in rural communities.

Despite the success of her endeavors with Kantha embroidery, Shamlu Dudeja faced a series of challenges and tragedies. The difficulties mounted when, within a span of one year, she tragically lost her son and husband to cardiac ailments. Diagnosed with a 7-pound tumor in her abdomen and later battling breast cancer, she grappled with health issues herself. These adversities tested her resilience and emotional strength. Yet, emerging from the depths of grief, Shamlu, akin to a phoenix, stood up with unwavering determination.

In a pivotal chapter of Shamlu Dudeja's life, a friend recognized her exceptional prowess in mathematics and offered sage advice that would resonate for years to come. Encouraged by her friend's insight, Shamlu embarked on the journey of writing mathematics books tailored for school children. Her dedication and proficiency in simplifying complex mathematical concepts led to the widespread adoption of her books in schools across India, Pakistan, and Sri Lanka. Though the educational landscape has evolved, with India and Sri Lanka moving away from her textbooks, Shamlu finds solace in knowing that her contributions endure. Notably, Pakistan continues to utilize her books, making her a respected figure in the educational realm. The royalties she receives not only validate the timeless relevance of her work but also serve as a source of contentment, bridging the years and preventing loneliness through the enduring impact of her intellectual legacy.

Along with working on her books, Shamlu redirected her focus towards Kantha too and decided to take her NGO, SHE Kantha, to unprecedented heights. The organization, with its motto 'Each one reach one,' became a catalyst for the revival of the Kantha culture. Shamlu's commitment went beyond personal setbacks, as she worked tirelessly to empower women both financially and emotionally. In this phase, she not only demonstrated her leadership in the Kantha revival but also showcased her dedication to uplifting communities through her NGO.

SHE Kantha's impact extended globally, adorning the creations on numerous famous personalities, including Mrs. Pratibha Patil, the past President of India, the Governor and Chief Minister of West Bengal, as well as ambassadors from various countries. Notably, the organization received 'The Community Impact Award' from the International Folk Art Museum in Santa Fe, adding to the recognition of Shamlu Dudeja's transformative work. Additionally, the visit of Hillary Clinton to SHE Kantha's stall in 2012 underscored the global acknowledgment of this ancient craft brought to the forefront by Shamlu's relentless efforts. Through SHE Kantha, Shamlu Dudeja not only revived Kantha embroidery but also provided a platform for local artisans to showcase their craftsmanship on the worldwide stage, leaving an indelible mark on the rich heritage of Bengal. What began as a personal appreciation for the artistry of Kantha artisans evolved into a mission to empower these local talents. Shamlu's decision to entrust them with silk sarees, and later, her active involvement in reviving the indigenous art form, highlighted her transformative impact on the lives of rural women.

This dual commitment to both mathematics education and the revival of Kantha embroidery showcased Shamlu Dudeja's versatility. By bridging the realms of academia and traditional craftsmanship, she not only enriched herself but also became a beacon of inspiration for others. Shamlu's journey exemplifies how a woman can transcend boundaries, excelling in diverse fields and making a lasting impact on both education and artisanal heritage.

The global recognition of Shamlu Dudeja's efforts in reviving Kantha embroidery and empowering rural women through SHE Kantha reached its zenith. The beautiful, multicolored creations crafted by the skilled artisans associated with SHE Kantha became sought-after treasures, adorning not only common individuals but also esteemed personalities. Shamlu's relentless dedication transformed her into a cultural ambassador, proving that a single woman's passion and perseverance can indeed bring about positive change on a global scale.

Taking a monumental leap in her life, Shamlu Dudeja demonstrated unparalleled courage and resilience. From the shores of Karachi to the vibrant corridors of Kolkata, her journey unfolded against the backdrop of historical events and personal triumphs. Faced with language barriers and societal challenges, she embraced change happily and courageously. Her advice to women considering a similar leap is rooted in her own journey – an unwavering belief in oneself, a willingness to embrace change, and a commitment to empowering others. She encourages women to break free from societal norms, pursue their passions, and not be daunted by challenges. Shamlu's life serves as a testament to the transformative power of resilience, creativity, and the pursuit of one's true calling.

In threads of time, a kantha tale unfolds,
Revivalist whispers, stories retold.
Needle and thread weave history's song,
A craft reborn, traditions prolong.
Hands that honor ancestral art,
Embroidering tales from the heart.
Kantha's revivalist, a steward of lore,
Stitching narratives, forevermore.
Patterns bloom like flowers in spring,
A dance of colors, memories cling.
Through every stitch, a legacy traced,
In the canvas of fabric, history embraced.
Threads intertwine, connecting past to now,
A revivalist's vow, a sacred vow.
Resurrecting beauty, a cultural reprise,

Kantha reborn, under skilled hands' ties.
In the needle's dance, a narrative spun,
Kantha's revival, a journey begun.
A craft reborn, in each careful endeavor,
A testament to art that endures forever.

4

Draping Seamless Elegance

Dolly Jain

***"With each fold and drape, a saree becomes a
canvas, and in the hands of a skilled drapist, it tells
a story of elegance, tradition, and the timeless
beauty woven into every thread"***

*She stood in front of her mother's full size bedroom mirror and
tucked the dupatta into her shorts. Bringing it around her
shoulder, she twisted and turned, trying to stand on her toes to
look at herself properly. What she saw, brought a wide smile
on her face. This was the third time she had draped the dupatta*

on herself that day but was she bored? Not at all! This routine of dressing herself like her mom had become a daily habit. Once she would get back from school, have lunch, finish her homework, this was her most favorite time of the day. The little girl was unknowingly, at such a young age carving a niche that was soon set to break records.

Indian women have broken age-old stereotypes and are rocking the professional scene. With a home, children and a million responsibilities to fulfill, they've still managed to emerge as superstars and do very well for themselves. Their relentless zeal, quench for success and hardwork is what sets them apart in this male dominated world. However, women today have demonstrated themselves in all sectors by overcoming serious challenges caused by gender bias and other social biases and cultural constructs. These women are pursuing unique paths and are doing remarkable things by contributing dynamically to the advancement of society and taking India by storm.

Born and brought up in Bangalore, Dolly grew up in a close knit family comprising of her parents and four siblings. Being the eldest among the five kids, she enjoyed supremacy and power but at the same time, loved and cherished the beautiful bond she shared with her three younger sisters and kid brother. Her parents raised all the kids in a way that prepared them to live fulfilled, happy and productive lives. For them, their children's academic performance did not matter as much as their outlook towards life. They taught all of them to be responsible individuals who needed to pursue something meaningful in life. Dolly's father was the most influential person for her, who taught the importance of being one's own boss. He always told her that it was fine to work under someone for sometime but everyone's final goal should be to become an entrepreneur, who would have many people working for her. Dolly carried this learning throughout her life and wholeheartedly owes her success to it.

Even though she could not pursue her studies for very long due to some unavoidable issues, she does not shy away from this fact and wants the world to understand that if she could achieve so much success without being academically strong, others can do too. She strongly believes that inspite of the several benefits education has, along with making us mentally strong, it doesn't mean that you need education to be successful. For success, one should have their goal set and remain focused towards it. Even if you are not educated enough, you can achieve great success in life by putting your skills in the right place and at the right time.

Dolly got married into an orthodox Marwari family where daughter in laws were supposed to dress up only in sarees. She used to hate wearing these as it would take her around 45 traumatic minutes to get ready everyday. She tried convincing her mother in law to allow her to dress in kurtas but all her pleading went in vain and she was left with no choice but to wear a saree every single day but what she did not know was, that this would one day, actually become the passion of her life. The girl who used to drape sarees around herself and her dolls during her growing up years, was now ready to drape sarees around women across the globe.

People would often compliment her on the way she wore her sarees and appreciated the way she carried the 6 yards with sheer elegance but Dolly's life took a huge turn the day she met veteran actor Late Sridevi. The latter lived in the same building as Dolly's maternal uncle and one day at a party, she happened to meet Sridevi who was struggling with her saree as she had spilt something on it. The saree lover Dolly offered to drape it for her and deftly began working on the pleats. Her expert finger movements were noticed by the late actor who simply commented – 'Why don't you take this up as a profession?' This question helped Dolly take the biggest leap in life.

Was it a cakewalk after this? No way, because as the daughter in law of a traditional marwari family, she had a lot of convincing to do. Dolly had decided to tread on a path that had never been chosen by anyone, therefore family, friends and the society thought her decision to be weird and silly. She soon became the center of discussion in her circle of friends and extended family because they all thought she will not be able to pursue her new found passion for long as draping a saree could never turn into a profession. But the dedicated, perseverant and ambitious Dolly had decided to prove them wrong and she took the leap.

Drape artist Dolly Jain is truly a force to reckon with, who has amazingly turned her passion into a successful profession and has made the saree an everyday fashion statement for women across the globe. Whether it is Natasha Poonawalla's Met Gala look, the Ambani weddings, Alia Bhatt's elegant wedding look, Katrina Kaif's bridal lehnga draping or dressing up beautiful brides and the other women in their families, Dolly is the one behind it all. She had set out with a challenge to encourage young girls to wear sarees and has accomplished it so well by putting the Indian garment on the global map. She is also the Guiness Book of Records holder for draping a saree in just 18.5 seconds and has been featured in the Limca Book of Records twice for draping the gorgeous attire in 325 different styles. At present, she is also working on a coffee table book with '365+1 styles of draping a saree' that'll help you drape a saree over a crop-top, jeans, skirt etc. You'll just need to name the drape and the book will have it for you.

As a professional drape artist for almost two decades, Dolly feels that it isn't the saree, the weave or the fabric many times, but what needs to be perfect is the underskirt or the petticoat and for this she has introduced the D'Coat which is stitched and designed to make the saree look and feel comfortable. Her initiative 'I Am by Dolly Jain' is revolutionizing the saree draping experience for women with just one solution – D'Coat that helps to create comfort and exude confidence. As the tattoo on Dolly's arm says, 'I am six yards ahead of my time', she has proved herself in more ways than one and all she wants is for women to not give up on their traditions, and the saree happens to be such a quintessential part of it.

Dolly Jain's story teaches that every challenge and hurdle that you cross takes you a step closer to your dream. So it is important to not give up and push forward even if it feels impossible sometimes. Women from all walks of life, have time and again showed us that the way to succeed is to hold on to your dreams and never give up. Everyday we are inspired by women who stand up for themselves and their beliefs as they chase their dreams. Each of these women didn't let the hurdles and the failures pull them down, and every time they have fallen, they have stood back up to chase their dreams.

In folds of fabric, where tradition is spun,
A saree drapist, an artisan under the sun.
With nimble fingers and an artist's grace,
They weave tales in pleats, a cultural embrace.
From silk to cotton, each fabric's tale,
In the gentle drape, stories set sail.
A symphony of colors, vibrant and bold,
In the saree drapist's hands, traditions unfold.
With skillful hands and patterns precise,
They paint a canvas, a garment's advice.
In every fold, a heritage worn,
A saree drapist, a culture adorned.
Around the waist, the saree's embrace,
They create elegance, a timeless grace.
A dance of pleats, a rhythm of threads,
A saree drapist, where tradition treads.
In ceremonial halls or daily streets,
They drape narratives, where heritage meets.
A saree's whisper, in every pleat,
A saree drapist, traditions repeat.
With artistry flowing, like rivers of silk,
They transform yards into cultural ilk.
In the language of fabric, a silent song,
A saree drapist, where traditions belong.

5

Against The Tide

Bula Choudhary

"From the quiet ripples of a childhood pond to the roaring waves of international seas, a journey that embodies the courage to dive into the unknown, the resilience to navigate challenging currents, and the determination to make a splash that echoes through the tides of history"

From the early days of her childhood, it was evident that she was destined for greatness in the water. At a tender age, she took her first strokes in a pond, wrapped in a thin towel instead of a conventional swimsuit. Little did anyone know that a budding champion was being nurtured. As her love for swimming grew, so did her aspiration to achieve something extraordinary in life. These humble beginnings laid the foundation for a remarkable journey that would see her overcome challenges and make waves in the world of competitive swimming.

Bula Choudhury, hailing from Hind Motors, West Bengal, had her initial tryst with swimming at the tender age of 2, under the guidance of her father. Their makeshift swimming spot was a pond just outside their house, where she would wear a thin towel (gamcha) in lieu of a conventional swimsuit. This unconventional yet determined start set the tone for Bula's aquatic journey. Her father, having faced a near-drowning incident in his youth, was resolute in teaching all his children the essential skill of swimming. Recognizing Bula's affinity for the water, he enrolled her in a club located two to three railway stations away, providing access to the River Ganga's swimming pool. It was here that a coach, on witnessing her innate swimming ability, predicted a remarkable future for the young Bula, setting the stage for her extraordinary sporting career.

As Bula Choudhury embarked on her formal swimming education at the club near the River Ganga, a pivotal moment in her journey unfolded during a challenging 7-mile swimming competition at the age of 6 and a half. Struggling with a cramp in her foot, she faced the harsh reality of not completing the race. The disappointed coach, initially impassive, stopped communicating with her. However, this setback proved to be a crucial turning point. Undeterred, young Bula apologized to her coach and pledged to finish all races moving forward. The following year, she stayed true to her promise, completing the race successfully. This early lesson taught her the invaluable truth that success often emerges from overcoming initial failures. Amid her pursuit of swimming excellence, Bula, one of five siblings, earned the affectionate nickname "chingri maach" (prawn) from those around her, showcasing her unique personality and resilience. Demonstrating prowess not only in swimming but also in athletics at the school level, Bula's multifaceted talent began to shine through, eventually leading her to a pivotal crossroads in choosing between athletics and swimming.

The crossroads in Bula Choudhury's life arrived when she had to make a significant choice between pursuing athletics or dedicating herself entirely to swimming. Opting for the latter, her mother's unwavering support became a crucial pillar of her journey. Despite residing 25 to 30 miles away from the swimming practice location, Bula's mother ensured her daughter's access to training, underscoring the family's commitment to her passion. This dedication bore fruit when, at the age of 8, Bula secured an opportunity to participate in the National level swimming competition in Chennai. Although she finished in the fourth position, just shy of her goal to secure the third spot, the experience left her disheartened but more determined than ever.

In response to this setback, Bula committed herself to rigorous training, practicing both in the morning and evening. A pivotal shift occurred when her family relocated to a new house, providing her with access to a pond. Undeterred by challenges such as practicing in the early morning darkness, Bula's resilience and dedication continued to grow. The subsequent year saw her participating in the National level competition in Bombay, where she clinched an impressive six gold medals at the age of 10, earning the title of junior National level champion. Her tenacity caught the attention of a German coach during a competition at Fort William when she was just 11, leading to her selection for the Indian camp in Patiala. This marked the beginning of Bula's remarkable journey on the international stage, overcoming adversities such as contracting chicken pox and emerging as the youngest member of the Indian team at the age of 12 during the Asian Games. Her unwavering commitment to her craft solidified her position as the National champion for an impressive decade.

In 1986, a significant chapter unfolded in Bula Choudhury's sporting career when an Australian coach entered the scene. Taking her to Australia for training, this marked a pivotal turning point that would shape the trajectory of her achievements. Despite already boasting an impressive array of medals, Bula found herself yearning for more challenges and greater accomplishments. This desire led her to venture into long-distance swimming in 1989.

Her determination and newfound focus catapulted her to remarkable achievements, including successfully crossing the formidable English Channel in the same year. This triumph marked the beginning of a series of extraordinary accomplishments, including winning the

81-km (50-mile) Murshidabad Long Distance Swim in 1996. Undeterred by challenges, Bula displayed her prowess by crossing the English Channel once again in 1999. However, her ambitions soared beyond familiar waters.

In 2005, Bula Choudhury etched her name in history by becoming the first woman to swim across sea channels off five continents. These channels included the challenging Strait of Gibraltar, the Tyrrhenian Sea, Cook Strait, Toroneos Gulf in Greece, the Catalina Channel off the California coast, and a swim from Three Anchor Bay to Robben Island near Cape Town, South Africa. Bula's feats in long-distance swimming not only showcased her unparalleled endurance but also demonstrated her ability to conquer diverse and demanding aquatic environments, solidifying her status as a trailblazer in the world of open water swimming.

With a strong belief in the 3D's – Dedication, Discipline and Devotion, Arjuna awardee and Padma Shree awardee Bula Choudhury gives a heartfelt message to aspiring young women with dreams of venturing into sports or swimming by reflecting on her own transformative journey. She emphasizes the importance of embracing challenges as stepping stones to success, drawing strength from setbacks, and finding resilience in the face of adversity. Bula encourages them to believe in their capabilities, to overcome self-doubt, and to nurture an unwavering commitment to their passion. She advocates for hard work, dedication, and the courage to dive into uncharted waters. Bula's message resonates as a beacon of inspiration, reminding these aspiring athletes that the journey may be challenging, but the rewards are worth every stroke.

In the azure expanse where waters gleam,
A legendary swimmer, a living dream.
With every stroke, a symphony of grace,
She navigates currents, a watery embrace.
In the pool's embrace, where ripples play,
A swimmer's journey takes its sway.
From the starting block to the finish line,
She dances with waves, a triumph so fine.
In each lap's rhythm, a heartbeat's song,
An athlete glides, the waters prolong.
With every kick and every breath,
She charts the course, conquering depth.
Beneath the surface, where silence reigns,
An award-winning swimmer breaks the chains.
Through lengths and laps, a story unfolds,
A journey of dedication, where tales are told.
In the echo of cheers and the pool's embrace,
A swimmer carves dreams, leaving a trace.
With medals gleaming, a testament bold,
She swims through victories, stories to be told.
From the blocks to podium heights,
An athlete's journey, where passion ignites.
In the water's ballet, where dreams shimmer,
An award-winning swimmer, a radiant glimmer.

6

Footprints of Impact

Mukta Nain

"In the fertile fields of knowledge, she cultivates minds, sowing seeds of curiosity, nurturing growth, and sculpting a future where the harvest is a bounty of empowered intellects and enlightened souls"

Even as a young girl growing up in Kolkata, she exhibited the seeds of leadership that would later flourish in her adult life. Attending school, she was not just a participant but a natural leader among her peers. Her carefree childhood, spent playing in the building compound and embarking on family vacations, showcased her affable nature and ability to connect with others. Even then, she displayed an innate sense of responsibility and decisiveness. The foundation for her leadership skills was laid during those early years, where she unknowingly honed the qualities that would define her success – a combination of confidence, a strong sense of responsibility, and a natural ability to inspire and lead others.

Mukta Nain's story began in the culturally rich city of Amritsar, Punjab, where she entered the world in December 1955. However, her journey took a turn when her father, a forward-thinking businessman, decided to move the family to Kolkata. This relocation was driven by his deep desire to ensure that his children received a top-notch education in the thriving educational environment of Kolkata. The decision set the stage for Mukta's formative years in the City of Joy, providing her with the opportunity to attend Modern High School, a prestigious girls' school known for its academic excellence. Mukta's childhood unfolded as a carefree and joyous period, marked by playful evenings with friends in the building compound and enriching family vacations orchestrated by her father. These early experiences laid the foundation for Mukta's later successes, shaping her perspective on education and life.

Mukta's journey took an unexpected turn when she discovered her passion for teaching during her pursuit of a Bachelor of Education (B.Ed). Realizing her natural aptitude and love for imparting knowledge, she took a leap of faith and found herself excelling in the role of an educator. Teaching not only became her profession but also a source of immense satisfaction as she recognized the profound impact she could have on shaping students' lives. Her time at the helm of education began to unfold organically, with each step contributing to her eventual role as the Principal of Birla High School.

Amidst her professional growth, Mukta acknowledged the crucial role her parents played in her life. A challenging phase emerged when she found herself taking care of her bedridden father, who battled Parkinson's Disease, and her ailing mother with a lung disorder. This period of balancing caregiving responsibilities with the demands of being a school principal was undoubtedly demanding. Yet, she approached it with resilience and managed to navigate through the complexities of a high-pressure job, demonstrating her ability to handle both personal and professional challenges simultaneously.

Her commitment and impact on the education sector were further validated when Mukta was honored with the Aparajita Award for Best Principal. This recognition, determined through online voting, underscored the positive influence she had on her students and the broader educational community. In her story, the intertwining threads of personal challenges and professional achievements highlighted her unwavering dedication and resilience in the face of adversity. This period further solidified Mukta's position as a formidable and inspiring figure, capable of navigating complex situations with grace and determination.

Reflecting on her life's journey, Mukta Nain attributed her success to a combination of dogged determination, common sense, and a keen ability to embrace and drive change. This mindset allowed her to navigate challenges, ensuring that her professional and personal life remained steadfast. Her success was not a result of complacency but stemmed from her willingness to try out new ideas and a commitment to experimentation. Believing in the inherent goodness of every individual, she demonstrated a positive and open-minded approach, fostering an environment of growth and learning.

Interestingly, Mukta revealed that no decision, even the choice to remain a confirmed spinster, was a difficult one for her. She viewed this decision as a conscious choice that provided her with the freedom and time to contribute more to society. Her ability to make decisions with confidence and purpose reflected a deep understanding of herself and her aspirations.

In contemplating a hypothetical restart, Mukta expressed a desire to delegate more responsibilities among capable individuals. This acknowledgment emphasized her belief in teamwork and effective delegation as essential components of successful leadership. Her advice to women contemplating their journey was simple yet powerful: "Jump! There is no gender bias or discrimination in today's world. Be prepared to conquer the world!" This sentiment encapsulated Mukta's outlook on life – one that encouraged courage, self-belief, and a proactive approach to challenges.

In essence, Mukta Nain's story was not just about her professional accomplishments but also about the mindset and principles that propelled her forward. Her resilience, adaptability, and the ability to make confident decisions shaped a narrative of success and positive impact.

Mukta Nain strongly believes in the importance of fair business practices, emphasizing the vitality of transparency, open communication, and equitable promotion procedures in the workplace. Her belief in fostering an environment built on fairness and integrity reflects not only her professional ethos but also her commitment to creating a positive and inclusive workspace.

Encouraging fair and transparent communication at all levels, Mukta advocates for a workplace culture that values every employee's input. By highlighting the significance of transparent promotion procedures, she aims to ensure that opportunities for career advancement are based on merit and devoid of biases.

Mukta's insistence on fair business practices is not just a professional stance but a reflection of her broader philosophy. She believes that these principles are essential not only for the success of an organization but also for the holistic well-being of its employees. Her advice serves as a reminder that ethical conduct and fairness are fundamental pillars for sustained success in any profession. This aspect of her story showcases not only her leadership philosophy but also her vision for a workplace that promotes ethical conduct and inclusivity.

Mukta Nain's story encapsulates a life guided by resilience, dedication, and a profound belief in the positive potential within every individual. Despite facing personal challenges while caring for her bedridden parents, Mukta managed to fulfill the demanding role of a school principal. Her ability to navigate through such a high-pressure situation showcases a remarkable strength and unwavering commitment to both her family and profession.

The intertwining threads of personal and professional challenges in Mukta's life reflect a narrative of balance and perseverance. Her dedication to education, evident from her time as a teacher to becoming the Principal of Birla High School, underscores a genuine passion for shaping young minds. Mukta's success in the educational sector, marked by accolades like the Aparajita Award, demonstrate the profound impact she has on the lives of students and colleagues alike.

Throughout her journey, Mukta embraced change and valued the ability to adapt. Her inner strength in the face of adversity, coupled with a positive mindset, became the driving force behind her success. Mukta's story serves as an inspiring example of how one can overcome challenges with determination, make meaningful contributions to society, and leave a lasting impact on the lives of those she touched.

In essence, Mukta Nain's life story is not just a chronicle of achievements but a testament to the power of perseverance, the pursuit of passion, and the impact one can have when driven by a genuine desire to make a difference.

In the hallowed halls where knowledge gleams,
An educationist weaves inspiring dreams.
A beacon of wisdom, guiding the way,
Igniting minds to brighten each day.
In classrooms echoing with curious minds,
A mentor's touch, where inspiration finds.

A symphony of lessons, a dance of thought,
An educationist's legacy, beautifully wrought.
With passion as ink, they script the lore,
In the book of learning, forevermore.
A canvas of minds, a palette of grace,
An educationist paints a vibrant space.
They plant seeds of curiosity and wonder,
Watch as intellects steadily thunder.
In the garden of academia, they tend,
Nurturing brilliance, to no end.
Through challenges faced, and triumphs embraced,
An educationist's spirit, never erased.
A journey of impact, a lifelong quest,
Their influence, a gift, forever blessed.
In the tapestry of learning, they play a part,
An educationist, a work of heart.
For in the corridors of wisdom they stand,
Crafting futures, with nurturing hands.

7

Skybound Dreams

Archana Kapoor

"Dreams take flight when passion becomes the unwavering pilot, navigating the currents of adversity with courage and determination"

In the enchanting corridors of her childhood, a young girl found herself captivated by the allure of the skies. It was a time when dreams were woven into the fabric of innocence, and the sheer vastness of the heavens above sparked her imagination. Gazing at the airplanes soaring majestically overhead, she felt a magnetic pull toward the limitless expanse of the sky. It was in these moments, perhaps fueled by the echo of her father's tales of aerial adventures, that a nascent dream took root within her tender heart – the dream to fly. In the quiet corners of her room, she would close her eyes and envision herself donning the distinguished uniform of a pilot, navigating the clouds with boundless freedom. Little did she know that these childhood musings would burgeon into a steadfast passion, setting the stage for a remarkable journey in the years to come.

Born in Delhi to an Air Force officer and a homemaker, Archana Kapoor's childhood emerges as a tapestry woven with the threads of love, support, and cherished family moments. These formative years laid the foundation for Archana's resilience, determination, and an enduring passion for flying. Her journey is intricately woven into the fabric of her upbringing and the close-knit bonds of her family. She fondly recalls the best times spent with her family – a big, loving unit that radiated warmth and support. The air was filled with laughter during holidays, and Archana cherishes those moments of joy and camaraderie shared with her father, his brothers, and their parents. It's within this familial embrace that her love for flying found its roots, nurtured by a collective passion for aviation that connected generations.

Amidst these cherished memories, Archana singles out her mother as the most influential person in her life. Her mother not only taught her how to think but also played a pivotal role in shaping her into the person she is today.

Reflecting on her childhood, Archana describes it as a time of simplicity and unbridled joy. Life was uncomplicated, and every moment carried a sense of happiness. In this idyllic setting, she found herself unconsciously drawn to the idea of wearing the pilot's uniform, a subtle manifestation of her deep-seated passion for flying. The unconditional backing of her family, coupled with the lessons instilled by her mother, became the bedrock upon which she built her dreams.

In the year 2009, the narrative of Archana Kapoor takes on a transformative hue. Now a Retired Squadron Leader, Archana stands as a testament to her unwavering commitment and groundbreaking achievements. Hailing from the first batch of Air Force women pilots in India, Archana not only realized her childhood dream but also successfully navigated a decade-long tenure in the Indian Air Force. What makes her story even more remarkable is her graceful transition from military service to a role in private carriers, highlighting her adaptability and versatility in the ever-evolving landscape of aviation. Archana's journey from a young dreamer enamored with her father's attire to a seasoned Squadron Leader exemplifies not only her personal triumph but also the broader shift in gender dynamics within the aviation industry.

As Archana Kapoor currently soars through the skies as a professional pilot with Vistara Airlines, her life unfolds as a testament to her enduring passion for flying. From her earliest memories, the desire to wear the pilot's uniform lingered in her subconscious, gradually shaping her aspirations. This intrinsic connection to aviation led her to pursue a career that would not only fulfill her dreams but also challenge societal norms.

Her journey was not without hurdles. When Archana joined the Air Force, she found herself not at the peak of physical fitness, and during the demanding training, doubts crept in. The rigorous regimen tested her resolve, and at times, the fear loomed large – a fear that she might not achieve her dream of becoming a pilot. It was during these challenging moments that her father's playful taunt, labeling her a "sissy" who couldn't make it, transformed into a catalyst for her determination. She embraced it as a challenge, vowing to prove that she could overcome adversity and live her dream.

Determination and drive became her companions on the journey, propelling her through the demanding training regimen and paving the way for her successful career. The lessons learned during this period of adversity – the importance of perseverance and self-belief – continue to shape her character as she navigates the skies in her current role.

Reflecting on her life, Archana emphasizes the significance of consistently discovering and rediscovering oneself. This introspective approach, coupled with an unwavering commitment to her dreams, has been crucial in her success. The passion that led her to the Air Force and the fulfillment of her childhood dream now serves as an inspiration to others, particularly women aspiring to break barriers in traditionally male-dominated fields.

Amidst the complexities of her personal and professional journey, Archana's story stands as a beacon of resilience, determination, and the triumph of dreams against the odds. Her advice to women echoes her own experience – to take the leap, embrace challenges, and witness how everything falls into place with unwavering commitment and resilience.

Archana Kapoor's life unfolds as a narrative of resilience and perseverance, not only in the professional realm but also in the personal challenges she faced. Amidst the simplicity and joy of her childhood, she encountered one of the most difficult periods post-marriage, realizing that she was entangled in a toxic relationship with her husband. This revelation marked a poignant chapter in her life, highlighting the complexities that coexist with personal pursuits and dreams. One of the most arduous decisions Archana had to make was related to motherhood. Discovering that she was expecting her second child while her first child was still very young presented a formidable choice. Despite her lifelong desire for two children, the circumstances compelled her to contemplate whether to proceed with the pregnancy. This decision-making process was undoubtedly emotionally taxing, yet Archana's ability to navigate such complexities speaks of her strength and resilience.

Through these trials, she emerged not only as an accomplished pilot but as someone who embraced life's challenges with courage and determination. The echoes of her experiences serve as valuable advice to others, especially women, urging them to take chances and confront obstacles head-on. Archana's belief that it's better to have tried and failed than not to have tried at all resonates as a testament to her philosophy of continuous self-improvement and the pursuit of personal growth.

Archana Kapoor's journey is encapsulated in her profound advice to women – to take the leap, discover and rediscover oneself, and embrace challenges with the assurance that everything else will fall into place. Her life has been a testament to the transformative power of determination, whether it was proving skeptics wrong during her Air Force training or navigating the complexities of personal relationships. Her unwavering commitment to her dreams, coupled with a genuine desire for self-discovery, has been instrumental in her success.

In skies where dreams ascend so high,
A daring spirit takes to fly.
With wings of steel and courage bright,
A pilot claims her flight.
Her gaze fixed on the vast expanse,
She soars with grace, a daring dance.
Through clouds and storms, she finds her way,
A trailblazer in the light of day.
Her hands upon the controls tight,
Navigating through the azure height.
A symphony of engines hum,
As she charts a course, her kingdom come.
In cockpit's realm, she wears the crown,
Defying gravity, she won't back down.
A trailblazer with passion's flame,
A pilot, in the sky, her name.

8

Achieve Your Dream, Change Your Destiny

Pinky Kapoor

"Through the gentle touch of compassion and the soothing balm of empathy, she transforms pain into strength, bringing the sacred art of healing to the hearts and souls of those in need"

"I can surely see name, fame and success for you but what I'm also sure of is that working in the kitchen and taking care of your home is not going to help you achieve that, so the question is what and how do I help you get closer to my prediction about you" murmured Kiran as she watched her sister tirelessly

working in the kitchen, quietly tending to everyone's whims and fancies. Kiran Kapoor, a renowned London based astrologer, always knew that behind the persona of a devoted housewife, hid a fabulous achiever who's destiny was about to change in a way that people would consult her to see positive changes in their own destiny. Her sister, who had never thought of being in a professional field was ready to see a renowned version of herself soon, just the way Kiran had predicted for her.

From gender equality to bridging the pay gap and having a voice, women are making us proud in all walks of life and its the best feeling to look up to another woman as a source of empowerment and strength. From managing homes to being a working woman, there are superwomen everywhere, truly making a change in the world we live in and continuing conversations that may have begun years ago but have taken all this time to be realized as important and not just something that can be forgotten about once the sun sets on the horizon.

Born in Delhi, Pinky was fortunate to have been brought up in the midst of caring and loving parents and siblings. Her elder brother Kuldeep was the most influential person in her life as he had answers to all the questions she put before him. Unfortunately, he passed away but his teachings and love still hold immense importance in Pinky's life. After completing her schooling from Ashok Hall Girls' Secondary School, she went on to pursue a BSc Honors degree in Homescience from J D Birla College. She soon got married to Mr. Harish Kapoor, an extremely understanding and affectionate man who showered immense love on the very elegant and petite Pinky. They were blessed with two beautiful kids – Sneha and Gaurav and Pinky took care of her family's needs without realizing the need of creating her own identity.

Pinky's sister Kiran who lived in London, always knew somehow that her sister was made to do greater things in life. Therefore, during one of her visits to London in the year 1999, she introduced Pinky to the world of Fengshui which was the latest fad in the European countries. Even though Pinky had never heard about the science of Fengshui, the books and magazines she collected to do some research on the subject, fascinated her tremendously. Along with her, Kiran's son Prashant was equally interested in the subject too and with him, Pinky began to delve deeper into it. Meanwhile, Kiran introduced her to one of her friends who was a very knowledgeable person and had almost mastered the science. He shared some more information with her and thus began Pinky Kapoor's journey of creating a name and identity for herself.

Pinky Kapoor was almost 40 years old when she decided to take the leap of faith and pursue something that she was set out to do always. As per Mark Twain's quote, "Age is an issue of mind over matter, If you don't mind, it doesn't matter." Pinky Kapoor is a woman who has achieved significant success and happiness in the later years of her life. From being a home body always, she did find it difficult initially to visit sites, houses, offices etc to check the places as per Fengshui but as people started recognizing and appreciating her work, they kept recommending her to their friends and families, and she's never looked back after that.

Once she was established in her profession, she took another leap when she was offered a half page weekly column in The Telegraph newspaper. This continued for 12 long years and in between, she was also given a full page coverage by Ananda Bazar Patrika which helped her get through to many prospective clients. Thereafter, her phone continued ringing for three days as new clients were trying to get in touch with her. Her career then took off to reach greater heights as her clients started getting good results and the fortunes of many people began changing for the better. She strongly believes that God is an invisible magician who has been doing wonders in all the houses she has visited and his grace and magic continues till date. In due course of time, Pinky received an offer from renowned Rupa & Co to write a book, which she co-authored with her nephew Prashant Kapoor and it got released in 2003. The book consists of true case studies, excerpts of personal experiences of people who have used and benefitted from Fengshui. It opens up a world of magic, mystique and miracles and is packed with magical tips and mystical remedies that can surely bring miraculous changes to every facet of one's life.

Besides her immense knowledge about Vastu and Fengshui, Pinky Kapoor specializes in Pillars Of Destiny, a powerful Chinese astrology. She is one of the very rare practitioners who has combined both the art forms and has been practicing the same for over 2 decades. She has also given a number of lectures and addressed several seminars in large gatherings such as

The Rotary, Ladies Study Group, Round Table, Conferences organized by The British High Commission, The Taj and Oberoi Group of Hotels to name just a few. Her career has taken her all across the globe to cater to clients. She specializes in residential and commercial spaces and provides consultations to offices, homes, hotels, resorts, factories, hospitals, shopping malls and showrooms, along with giving personal consultations to individuals including detailed analysis of their horoscopes. She also conducts workshops for women interested to take up Vastu, Fengshui etc as their profession.

We women always need motivation to take that leap and move forward in life. Pinky Kapoor's story ensures a strong dose of inspiration and can help you ultimately be the person you want to be. She strongly believes that you should do what you love. It takes courage, passion and commitment to go after what you really want and it can be stifling to be associated with something you don't resonate to. So trust your instincts, stay true to your own beliefs, take the leap of faith and pursue what you love the most and success will follow suit.

In the realm where souls find solace and light,
A spiritual healer, a guide in the night.
With hands that channel energies unseen,
They weave healing whispers in a serene sheen.
Amidst the cosmos, where energies align,
A healer's touch, a balm for the divine.
In the dance of chakras, a sacred ballet,
They harmonize spirits, leading the way.
Through the ether of prayers and incense swirls,

A spiritual healer, where transcendence unfurls.
With wisdom as old as the ancient trees,
They nurture the spirit, setting it free.
In the tapestry of aura, colors unfold,
A healer's presence, a sanctuary bold.
With every chant, a mantra's grace,
They offer serenity, a celestial embrace.
In the quiet moments, where healing springs,
A spiritual healer, their essence sings.
A bridge to realms where energies flow,
They guide the lost, helping them grow.
With hands that carry the weight of the divine,
A healer's journey, where souls intertwine.
In the cosmic ballet, a healer's role,
A conduit for healing, making spirits whole.

9

Life is a miracle

Nehha Fatehpuria

Albert Einstein had once said, "There are only two ways to live your life. One is as though nothing is a miracle. The other is as though everything is a miracle"

Many of us believe in the same and there are many who believe that miracles happen to those who believe in them. Isn't there so much more to life than what we actually see? Strange positive things happen when they are not supposed to and that is the time life changes for the better and not only for ourselves but also for those connected to us. When we all need miracles in our lives at some point or the other, don't we also need angels who could facilitate our journey towards those magical moments of happiness and contentment. These angels help us to interpret messages of that divine guidance and bring more happiness and peace into our lives and in the world around us too. These healers or angels as I would prefer calling them can sometimes act as antidepressants and they have the power and the ability to motivate and empower people to move forward with their lives and achieve their goals.

Born and brought up in a beautiful and happy family in Jaipur India, who knew back then that this young girl would one day transform lives and become the point of communication between the receiver and not only the guardian angels but also other types of healing modalities. While playing innocently around the house with her siblings, this chirpy young girl was set to change the world with positivity.

Spending her life in a joint family, Nehha Fatehpuria knew how to share, adjust and live in harmony. She has two brothers – one elder and one younger and was therefore the favourite of her father. He made sure to instill philanthropic values in his kids from a very young age. He always believed in serving humanity and taught them to do the same as well. Even though she belonged to a middle class family, her dad was famous for helping people around in whatever way he could. People knew him as a person who did not know how to say 'no' and Nehha feels this is one value that she has taken from him in the best possible way.

As she grew up and got married into an orthodox Marwari family, where all members were supposed to follow a certain set of rules, life could have been similar to that of a normal daughter in law of any family, but Nehha's in-laws allowed her to choose a career of her choice at the age of 31 and she even flew all by herself to pursue her teachers programming. This was the first big leap she took in her life and from being a part of a conservative family, she was now on her own in the magnificent United States, all set to pursue her dreams. Once she was back from the US, she was fortunate to find her mentor who she felt was there to guide her to achieve greater heights but life had other plans. And soon she understood that the beautiful relationship she shared with her was short lived and one sided. Nehha considered her to be her blood sister, sacrificed everything to help her, be with her, even if that meant leaving her small kids alone at home just so that she could learn more from her but the day she decided to begin her own journey as a healer and mentor, she completely disowned Nehha to the extent of maligning her and challenged her abilities to do anything independently. This was an extremely dark phase of Nehha's life because someone whom she had looked upon as a teacher, healer, sister and guide was the reason behind her being demotivated and with decreased self confidence.

This was when she took the second leap in her life - the time she decided to move on without her mentors guiding light. Today when she looks back, Nehha does realise the importance of that. Because the heartbreak taught her to be self dependent and to follow the path that had been crafted for her. Another teacher who she had always looked up to, advised her to just forgive and let her go and once Nehha followed this advice, her life became much better and she started her healing group called Lightworkers of Angels. She hasn't looked back since then and owes all her growth with immense gratitude to the people who have showered their unconditional love on her and her work.

Nehha is grateful that once she took the second leap in her life, she transformed into an intuitive, clairvoyant and powerful energy healer and therapist. She began coaching, mentoring and guiding her clients through clearing their core issues, limiting beliefs and deeply rooted energetic blocks that keep them stuck from living a more fulfilled life. She realised that she had slowly become a detective for people who were unable to figure out what was wrong with them.

Nehha started understanding how her life was like a thread in a great tapestry woven together with everyone else and how every action that she took was perfect and served a purpose. She says that the question we all need to ask ourselves is 'who am I'. As we go on a journey to discover who we are, a purpose will slowly unfold before us. When we go through hardships in life, it is absolutely necessary to love yourself and to know you are worthy and deserving of good things because once we know we have a purpose, our body starts to reflect that.

Like many of us, Nehha's life has been a long and difficult journey. However, if there's one thing she knows, it's that no matter how you feel or how your life is, you have the power within you to create a better version of yourself and your life. Her willingness to take that leap opened new doors for her and she's sure every jump you take will increase your wisdom and broaden your vision.

Most of us, at some point in our lives have taken leaps of faith. We've done things outside the realm of our comfort in an effort to get somewhere else or grow in some way. There is no formula for determining whether the leap is a little one or a big one. What is a small step for one person might be another persons big leap and vice versa. What Nehha saw as disappointment in her chosen path was actually the leap that opened new opportunities for her. So extend your ability to experience positive things and allow yourself to savor the good that happens to you.

In the sanctuary where spirits find reprieve,
A spiritual healer, their presence weaves.
With hands that channel ethereal might,
They guide souls toward healing's light.
In realms unseen, where energies align,
A healer's touch, a seraphic sign.
Whispers of mantras, an ancient hymn,
They navigate realms where spirits swim.
Through the corridors of the metaphysical,
A spiritual healer, transcending the physical.
In the dance of auras, an ethereal ballet,
They balance energies, leading the way.
With sage and crystals, tools of the trade,
A healer's craft, in shadows and shade.
Through the veil of illusions, they gently part,

Guiding seekers toward the heart.
In the stillness where intentions bloom,
A spiritual healer dispels the gloom.
A conduit for wisdom, a beacon so bright,
They bring forth healing, dispelling the night.
With an open heart and a knowing gaze,
A healer orchestrates cosmic displays.
In the dance of healing, a soulful art,
They mend the fragments, repairing the heart.

10

Beauty At Her Fingertips

Bridgette Jones

"When virtue and modesty enlighten her charms, the lustre of a beautiful woman is brighter than the stars of heaven, and the influence of her power it is vain to resist"

"Dear Santa, may I please get the latest set of hair cutting scissors for Christmas this year? I really like the ones Susan aunty has and I promise I'll always be a good girl" wrote the young girl.

"What are you writing sweetheart? Oh, a letter to Santa. What do you want from him this year? Asked her mom.

"I've asked him for a set of scissors."

"But what happened to the set you have?"

"It's outdated mum...Susan aunty at the salon has really lovely ones and I've requested Santa to get me those" she said with a smile."

The little girl was 10 years old and almost ready to carve her niche in the cosmetology world.

As time changes, the rise of female entrepreneurs in India has shown that women in business are capable of matching the success of their male counterparts. Especially in a country that is deeply patriarchal in several areas, its not just difficult but challenging for female entrepreneurs. Women here are still considered to be emotional, less ambitious and not supposed to lead an initiative and turn it into a profit-making business. But, the fact is that women are no longer held bound by this perception. They are equivalent to males when it comes to starting or running a profitable business. And we know this because we have seen it.

Born and brought up in Kolkata, Bridgette's family consisted of six members – her parents, a brother, two sisters and herself. They had a close knit family with never a dull moment ever. Both her mom and dad were working, so Bridgette and her siblings were mostly brought up by their nanny, but they never missed the love and guidance of their parents, as they were always there to protect and nurture them in the best possible way. They had a lovely neighbourhood where they thoroughly enjoyed the company of other children living there. With no mobile phones and internet back then, they spent joyous days playing games such as hopscotch, hide and seek, 7 marbles and more. Bridgette completed her schooling from Loreto House – a premium institution in Kolkata known for instilling core values in all its students. Her years in school and the time she spent with her parents and siblings kept her grounded and helped her grow into a beautiful yet strong woman. A family oriented, hardworking and magnanimous man, Bridgette's father was the most influential person in her life, who kept her and the family safe and protected always. Along with him, her mom taught all the children strong and ethical moral values that have helped shape them into wonderful individuals.

After completing her education, Bridgette got married to Ronald, who till date has influenced and encouraged her tremendously. Soon after her marriage, she took up an office job during the week and started helping out in a salon on weekends. She had always nurtured a knack of hair cutting and styling and while her stint at the salon, she realized her innate talent and made up her mind to pursue it wholeheartedly. She was born as a left handed person but due to her perseverance, passion and commitment, she soon trained herself to work with her right hand too. At present, Bridgette can cut hair with both her hands, which is an extremely rare achievement. Once she had decided to pursue her childhood passion, she got enrolled into various courses to hone her skills. With the ability to bring her vision to reality, Bridgette has successfully created unique looks by taking inspiration from around her and using latest trends, tools, techniques and styles. From a very young age, she had an artistic eye and after all the years of sharpening her skills, she carries the potential of enhancing and beautifying people as per their requirements. Her expertise in the field has helped her attain a clear understanding of best suited styles, colors, textures etc and this is what has made her a people's favourite. People who get their makeover done by Celebrity Hair & Makeup Artist Bridgette Jones, always appreciate her work and most importantly they love that she beautifully turns their thoughts into reality.

Bridgette founded her own salon brand 16 years ago – Bridgette Jones Fashion Salon that has given her even more opportunities to express herself in several ways. She has dealt with competitions and various challenges but they have all made her a strong entrepreneur. She believes that every client who walks through her door, is an opportunity for creativity and innovation. Whether it is a simple color or a trendy haircut, each client goes from a work in progress to a work of art. The best part is that her work makes her a part of all major events in her clients' lives whether it is marriage, birthday or graduation. Her entrepreneurship journey has not been a smooth one but with the support of her husband and two gorgeous daughters, she has managed to sail through it all. She has got many celebrities and socialites in her long list of clientele and has managed to keep them all on top priority and has never failed to wow them through her exceptional talent. She feels that everyone dreams to look like an ideal star while sitting on her salon chair and she helps them to own that look.

Creativity, resilience and remarkable stories, the superpowers in women have persistently created stories that exemplify the ultimate power of womanhood hood while adding charm to their unique existence. Passionately making ends meet and fiercely creating history in their own world, females are working relentlessly to structure their ideas and ambitions. Bridgette Jones took a leap in life when she realized her innate ability to make women look even more gorgeous and slowly her expertise captivated the attention of many across the globe. She has successfully carved a niche for herself that has reinvented the Hair & Makeup world. Her prominence and creativity has been impressing people around her and her presence has inspired various young hustlers too, waiting to take that leap. She urges women to fight against all odds, societal stigma and stereotypes to emerge as winners with a smile on their face.

In the canvas of faces, where beauty unfolds,
A cosmetologist's touch, a tale to be told.
With brushes that dance like whispers of air,
They paint confidence, a radiance so fair.
In the tapestry of transformation, they weave,
A symphony of colors, a visual reprieve.
From contouring shadows to hues that gleam,
They sculpt self-esteem, like an artist's dream.
In the realm of salons, where mirrors reflect,
Cosmetologists craft, with skills perfect.
From manicured nails to a coiffure divine,
They redefine beauty, where features entwine.
With potions and lotions, a magic concoction,

They nurture the skin, an artful devotion.
A cosmetologist's hands, a soothing caress,
In the beauty industry's dance, they impress.
Through every snip and every brushstroke,
A transformation emerges, a beauty bespoke.
With every client, a canvas anew,
A cosmetologist's art, a masterpiece true.
In the symphony of scissors and vibrant hues,
They create confidence, dispelling the blues.
A cosmetologist's touch, where beauty takes flight,
In the mirror's reflection, a radiant light.

11

Closing deals in heels

Mamta Binani

***"She is clothed with strength and dignity, and she
laughs without fear of the future"***

*Running around open grounds and narrow lanes, enjoying the
Kalbaisakhi rain, aiming at the ripe mangoes on the large tree
in the backyard, or imitating the Nirma ad girl for the
umpteenth time in a day, her early days were replete with a fine
mixture of happiness, joy and affection. This young girl had a
very playful childhood because of the neighbourhood she lived
in. There were many kids her age and they would run around*

the grounds, lush greenery, open terrace and the bylanes carefree and happy. From playing hide and seek to aptly aiming marbles into holes, she captured all these moments into her soul.

Women throughout history have shared great knowledge and wise thoughts with a multitude of generations. Now more than ever, women in business, entertainment, professionals and everything in between recognise the importance of lifting each other up to thrive and succeed in success. Such women also understand the growing need to empower one another to be brave in the face of fear. Women today are in senior authoritative positions, they are CEOs, entrepreneurs, philanthropists and much more. Their innovation, dedication and compassion allow them to be great leaders and inspire the next generation to reach greater heights than ever before.

Born and brought up in a family where virtues such as discipline and flexibility were at the forefront, Mamta Binani learnt all the mantras to remain happy and successful, from a very early age. Her family instilled values such as giving and sharing, along with imbibing forgiveness and simplicity, and teaching her to stay light and stress-free always. Her father taught her to remain calm and poised in extreme situations and to never carry any negative emotions in her heart beyond the day. Alongside, she imbibed the skillsets of treating guests in the best possible way from her mother, who also taught her to be caring and compassionate.

Mamta is a practising lawyer with a specialisation in corporate and insolvency laws. Prior to this, she practised as a company secretary. She likes to call herself a bold person but not very talkative when it comes to gossiping or discussing matters related to jewellery, clothes etc. But if she finds herself in the midst of people discussing policies, politics and general subjects of relevance, then she's quick, precise and sure to put her point forward. Having given more than 4500 lectures till date, she has received immense applause and accolades for her speaking skills.

Mamta feels lucky and fortunate to have found unconditional support from her spouse, who has been one of the most influential people in her life, apart from her parents and teachers. She also owes her success to her mother-in-law and daughter who have always been very understanding and have helped her to march forward as they never created impediments.

Brave, fierce and perseverant, Mamta isn't afraid of the challenges or tribulations she faces once in a while. She's taken them all with a pinch of salt and considers these minor setbacks and obstacles as self defining and character strengthening exercises. Even though, it was initially difficult for her to create a name and space for herself in the industry, but her attitude of treating work as worship and every client as God, has made her triumphant.

Mamta owes her success to her ability to stick to things and not give up. She has a strong will to stay awake and valid and to never consider herself sub optimal or substandard. She believes that discipline is one factor responsible for anybody's success. For her, intelligence is not a barometer because one has to have a logical point of mind and the rest is input deciding the output. Money has never been a driving force for her and she has always strived to compete with herself all the time.

Mamta Binani took a major leap in life when she decided to pursue her dream of becoming her own boss. It always intrigued her to have an office with a chair designated to no one else but her. Having made that dream come true, she considers herself extremely fortunate and blessed. The day she decided there was no tomorrow, she set out to achieve her dream of becoming her own boss. She strongly believes that every time is the right time to take a leap. Opportunities do not come knocking always so it's your job to simply take the plunge and learn to swim when in water. Remember desperation teaches everything and even the art of balancing. Try and carve a niche for yourself and you will slowly and steadily find yourself reaching your goal. Every woman is strong, so don't sit around feeling sorry for yourself, nor let people mistreat you. If you fail, you will rise up even stronger because you're a survivor, not a victim. You are in control of your life and there is nothing you cannot achieve.

In the courtroom's hush, where justice prevails,
An inspiring lawyer, her story unveils.
With eloquence that dances like a legal waltz,
She fights for truth, where justice exalts.
A guardian of rights, in the legal arena,
She navigates complexities with a gaze so keen.
In the tapestry of law, her arguments unfurl,
A defender of justice, an empowering whirl.

From the scales of balance to the gavel's decree,
She stands as a beacon, strong and free.
In the corridors of justice, where ethics guide,
Her voice resonates, a legal tide.
With every case, a narrative untold,
Her advocacy a testament, a story bold.
Through the labyrinth of laws, she charts a course,
An inspiring lawyer, a legal force.
In the pursuit of truth, where principles reign,
Her convictions echo, a clarion refrain.
A defender of rights, in the legal strife,
She stands as a pillar, the embodiment of life.
An inspiring lawyer, where rights find voice,
In the realm of justice, her spirit poised.
With every argument, a chapter penned,
A legal luminary, inspiring to the end.

12

A Warrior Princess

Shobhika Kalra

"Embracing life's journey with wheels that turn dreams into triumphs, she exemplifies strength, resilience, and the undeniable power of a spirit that knows no bounds"

At first glance she hated the sight of the wheelchair and the more she looked at it, her anger and hatred knew no bounds. It took time for her to realize that she was not an ordinary girl, as she was someone who had come into this world to achieve the extraordinary. Slowly she overcame all the negativity and started looking at life with an all new perspective. During one of her visits to India, she and her sister went to watch a movie. She had to be carried into the cinema hall because they did not have a ramp for wheelchairs. They realized that even UAE had very few ramps and that's when they decided it was time to bring about a change. The girl who was carried into the cinema hall was made from a concoction of grit, determination, strength, courage and lots more.

When it comes to inclusion, the world still has a long way to go in making way for people with disabilities. From daily challenges to the stigma that differently abled face, we need to undergo a complete transformation. The biggest push for change has come from people who have faced the challenges themselves. Even though they have gone through various ups and downs in their journey, a few women like Shobhika Kalra who themselves have suffered disability, are ferociously supporting their cause and creating awareness. Women like her are a source of inspiration. In the face of disability and the challenge and stigma attached to it, they have taken up the mantle of change and not only re-invented their lives but went on to change the lives of others as well.

Born in Delhi, Shobhika soon shifted to UAE with her parents and elder sister. Her tryst began when at the tender age of 13 she was diagnosed with a rare degenerative nervous system disorder that back then shattered her life completely. Prior to this, Shobhika was a topper in academics and extra-curricular activities. Life was good but then it had other plans. She shut herself inside her room for two years and it was not only a trying time for her but also for her family who were finding it extremely hard to come to terms with her condition.

Despite the trauma she went through due to her disability, she managed to beat all odds to finish school, complete a bachelors degree in Business Management and a Masters degree in Psychology. In the year 2014, she launched an initiative called 'Wingz of Angelz' to make the world more wheelchair accessible. Her enterprising venture is a disability awareness group that works with organizations to help construct ramps in public places. Due to the initiative taken by Shobhika, Wingz of Angelz has made 1000 places in Dubai more wheelchair accessible. At present, Shobhika is the youngest Indian in the Middle East to receive the 'She The Change' – Udyami Award. Alongwith this, she is also a TikTok 'fluencer and a disability model.

With a strong will and a positive mindset, Shobhika makes it a point to make each day happy. She knows that the path she chose to walk on is still not something that has been discovered by many people, therefore she took a major leap in life when she decided to choose to do things her way and not get bogged down due to perceptions of people who were trying their best to not let her trust her capabilities.

Shobhika is grateful to her broad minded and supportive family who have always made sure that she believed in herself and do the extraordinary. The hardest decision of her life was to decide whether to have a personal life or work towards helping people like herself. She chose the latter but even though it seemed tough back then, she is extremely glad she took that leap.

With eyes as bright as a shining star and a smile that can light up people's lives, Shobhika is a determined and ambitious girl who is the perfect example to prove that disability is just a state of mind. Her ability to put aside her issues and think about how she could benefit the society is truly inspirational. She proves that despite the issues one may face in life, happiness is something that is a real possibility. The level of limitations you experience may be massive but there is certainly hope in each day. The key to happiness is choosing to maintain a positive outlook on life itself. People with disabilities are contributing members to society like everyone else and their skills and abilities are just as valuable as anyone else's skills and abilities.

Shobhika's story tells everyone that the next time you feel bogged down by any hardship, remember to rise above it and create a smooth path not only for yourself but for others too. She did not see her disability as an insurmountable obstacle but as a challenge that would push her to achieve great things. She did not focus on what life had taken away from her but rather on what life had to offer. She learnt and is now teaching people across the world, how to not only adjust to life in a wheelchair, but to triumph, no matter the odds.

In the realm of challenges, where courage resides,
A girl on wheels, strength in her strides.
In the echo of wheels on a path unexplored,
A world she creates, her spirit adored.

A wheelchair, not a hindrance but a chariot of might,
She navigates obstacles with a determined light.
Through each spin, a trailblazer's quest,
Creating a haven where all can find rest.
Inaccessible norms, she seeks to redefine,
A world of possibilities, uniquely designed.
Her dreams, an architect's grand scheme,
Building bridges where others may dream.
With resilience as her compass, determination her guide,
She carves pathways where inclusivity abides.
In the tapestry of challenges, her story unfolds,
A symphony of strength, a tale to be told.
She paints a world where acceptance thrives,
A kaleidoscope of dreams, where everyone thrives.
Through each roll, an anthem of grace,
A girl on wheels, creating her space.
In her world, barriers crumble and fall,
As she weaves a narrative, breaking down walls.
A testament to fortitude, a beacon so bright,
A girl on wheels, creating a world just right.

13

Life Is Art, Live Yours in Colour

Surabhi Agarwal

"There is something beautiful about a blank canvas, the nothingness of the beginning that is so simple and breathtakingly pure. It's the paint that changes its meaning and the hand that creates the story"

There is truly something magical about getting close to a painting. It makes you feel so utterly engrossed in the minimalistic of details that you tend to forget that the work in front of you is a physical manifestation of someone's vision and talent. It is said if you wish to shake up your own view of the universe, you need to step into the inner life of an artist who'll make you see your surroundings in the most unique and beautiful way. The vast freewheeling swathes of the artist's paintbrush sweeps the onlooker and takes them on a journey or a rollercoaster ride across the canvas and drowns them into the intense colours that 'pop' against one another in a playful or reckless way. It seems as if the colours on the canvas are having a dialogue with each other, while also attracting others to join in the conversation. The painting procedure is always empirical where each stroke followed by another leads to the narration of a wonderful story waiting to be told to the world.

"Who's this?" asked the chirpy 7 year old.

"He is a famous personality", replied her mum.

Both mother and daughter stood on the roadside looking at the statue of a renowned freedom fighter of India.

"I'll have my statue here when I grow up", said the little one.

Her mom smirked, "Why will anyone place your statue here?"

"Because I'll be famous too…I'll be a great artist when I grow up."

The 7 year old was Surabhi Agarwal, a bubbly but ambitious girl who at that innocent age knew she had to make it big in life. How and what was unknown.

Born in Kolkata in a huge joint family where her cousins were her best friends and she was thoroughly pampered by one and all. Her elder sisters were more like her mother, friends, philosophers and guides. They were instrumental in giving her the wind beneath her wings and urged her to pursue all that her heart desired to do.

Even though she was encouraged to follow her heart, deep within she was still the quintessential Indian girl who felt it was her duty to seek permission from her elders before taking any decision. She always felt permission or approval was necessary from her parents, elder siblings or later on from her husband and in-laws too.

At a very young age and because of a keen interest in art, Surabhi had nurtured a dream of pursuing architecture but back in those days, this was not one of the popular subjects students would opt for, therefore she was discouraged and advised to follow the path others were walking on.

As luck would have it, she got married as soon as she completed school and along with her husband, went to Australia to pursue graduation. Once they were back in India and she began her duties as a daughter-in-law, she got immensely occupied in daily household chores. Art and paints were still an important part of her life that she would practice quietly and discreetly in some corner of the house.

A year later, she was blessed with her son and eventually became even more occupied in not only household chores but also in bringing him up. Her passion for art became a mere hobby where she would only create artwork to give as gifts among family and friends.

After her son was a few years old, she conceived again but sadly due to some complications, she had a miscarriage which left her extremely heartbroken and depressed. She never took professional help but her state was so bad that it was a challenge to even wake up each day. Her son was the only reason she could rely on to make her live life again. Along with his company, she also found solace in painting and gradually came out of the low phase. What started as a step to find strength to stand up, had now given her wings to fly.

She had no clue that back then the little solace she got from painting on canvas would finally turn out to be the leap in life that was to take her ahead to help her pursue her passion. Even though she found a partner in art, she still had to keep it all hidden from her family as according to most of the people around her, this was not a career that someone could wish to pursue. But, while listening to all the advice that came to her from all corners, she was adamant to do what was giving her utmost happiness and realized that she had finally found her calling. There was absolutely no looking back then. She knew that she had to take charge of her life and let bygones be bygones.

By then, she had already managed to have a decent collection of her artwork which she had passionately created, away from the prying eyes of people. She connected with a few other artist friends and together they decided to put up an exhibition. She was extremely lucky to receive an amazing response and managed to sell off most of her paintings. Her family thought this was it and she obviously would not take the trouble of painting anymore. What they saw was an exhibition hall where all paintings were sold out but what they failed to see was the new and unstoppable Surabhi who was gaining motivation from the empty hall.

Surabhi kept painting and went on to showcase each of them in solo and group exhibitions along with various pop-up shows and received immense appreciation from clients across India and worldwide too. She was happy to evoke her emotions on canvas where she tried to create poetry through the strokes of her brush.

Creativity and art is something that comes from within Surabhi Agarwal and once she had taken that leap to pursue her passion, she knew this was her inner calling. To help her follow her love for art, she was and is extremely fortunate to have her husband as her biggest supporter. He has always encouraged her to have confidence in herself. From the time they got married, he would make it a point to discuss business matters with Surabhi and happily took her advice every now and then and it's all because of him that she has now started assisting him in his work as well. **Surabhi believes the best possible thing you can get out of a relationship is that you're with someone who encourages you to be the best version of yourself every day.** She feels lucky that her partner created a beautiful space for her to do what she wanted to do the most and she truly loves and respects him for that.

Surabhi never studied art as a subject but once she decided to take it up professionally, she trained under art maestros such as the very renowned and legendary artists Suvaprassana for sculpture and Luxma Goud for etching. She strongly believes that the art which comes from within the heart is the one that connects with the connoisseurs the most. She has time and again brushed up her skills by following some of the great artists our country has given birth to. She is a true Indian and the same can be seen in all her paintings where she tries to fuse Indian aesthetics with contemporary art. She is a strong supporter of gender equality and this is the reason why you will notice a celebration of feminity and womanhood in most of her artworks.

She is blessed with a strong following of Indian and international clientele who have appreciated and loved her work. Through her paintings, she has tried to depict the various emotions of women who have been under the bondage of our society. Art is Surabhi's way of connecting to people and depicting what is going on around her. Through her art, she tends to express her thoughts on diverse topics, women empowerment being one of them.

Last year, when the whole world was struggling through the pandemic situation, art kept her busy and she was fortunate to have tons of work that helped her to remain sane. During the lockdown situation and when Kolkatans were wondering whether they would get a chance to celebrate Durga Puja, she decided to come up with a series on our city of joy and she vividly used her creativity and imagination to create some stunning pieces that depicted the life in our city. Through her artwork, she portrayed the undying spirit of Kolkata where even though the lanes were devoid of any activity and the people were unsure of what would happen, deep within we all knew that the city would be back with its undying love and spirit for festivities.

She strongly believes that if she could take that much required leap in life to follow her heart and passion, anyone can. Many women struggle to muster that faith to take that leap, to risk the safety of where they are now for the possibilities they want most, but one just needs to follow their heart and truly believe in themselves. There is nothing that women cannot achieve. Never doubt your capabilities. So bet on yourself, defy those inhibitions, take that leap and in the end, you'll be so glad you did it.

In the realm of creation, where visions abound,
An artist emerges, where dreams are found.
With brushes dipped in colors bold,
They paint stories untold, a canvas to unfold.
In the quiet of a studio, where silence speaks,
An artist's spirit, creativity peaks.
From strokes of passion to hues that sing,
They give life to thoughts on a whispering wing.
In clay's embrace or with pencils fine,
An artist's touch, a gift divine.
Sculpting worlds from thoughts profound,
They weave magic, where imagination's crowned.
From the dance of shadows to the play of light,
An artist captures moments, both day and night.
In each stroke, emotions run,
A gallery of feelings, a masterpiece spun.
With hands that sculpt and fingers that trace,
An artist breathes life into empty space.
Through the palette of emotions, a vivid chart,
They create symphonies, a visual art.
In galleries adorned with dreams set free,
An artist's creations, a tapestry.
A storyteller with colors, a visionary's flight,
They paint the world in sheer delight.

14

Harmony of Empowerment

Kavita Agarwal

"From humble beginnings to empowering others, the journey is a melody of resilience and embracing one's true calling"

Even as a young girl, she harbored ambitions that transcended the boundaries of traditional expectations. She would often envision a future where women could break free from societal confines. She dreamt of a world where women, like herself, could realize their full potential beyond predefined roles. The seeds of her passion for women empowerment were sown early, sprouting from the belief that every girl, regardless of societal expectations, deserved the opportunity to shape her destiny. Little did she know that these early aspirations would blossom into a lifelong commitment, culminating in the creation of a community dedicated to empowering women and rewriting the narratives that had once confined her own dreams.

In the bustling streets of Kolkata, amidst the clamor of daily life, this little girl's story began in the embrace of a humble family. Born to simplicity, she thrived in the warmth of a joint family setup, sharing a small flat with 20 relatives. Amidst the daily hustle, her fondest memories were woven into the fabric of close-knit relationships, especially with her 11 cousins who became her companions in joy and support. Sundays were a special affair, marked by the savory aroma of chowmein, expertly prepared by one of her cousins, a tradition that became a symbol of familial togetherness.

Education, the cornerstone of Kavita's upbringing was a value instilled by her father from the very beginning. In the midst of the joint family chaos, routines were crafted for holidays, delicately balancing studies and play.

As the youngest among the cousins, Kavita reveled in the vibrant tapestry of festivals guided by her elder cousins. Each celebration became a lesson in unity, cultural richness, and the strength derived from familial bonds. The simplicity and hard work that surrounded her upbringing was to later echo in her own journey.

With parental influence as her compass, Kavita stepped into the world with a mindset molded by discipline and hard work. Her life took a turn when she married Samir, a man who embodies these values and is a paragon of diligence.

However, the turning point arrived when Kavita realized the untapped potential within her during her 20-year stint in investment banking. Working alongside her husband, she sensed a dormant ambition and desire for personal identity. The perception of her role as a mere pastime struck a chord, leading her to question her own aspirations and the societal norms that confined her.

Amidst the triumphs, Kavita reflects on the most challenging period of her life—the aftermath of her first child's delivery. Faced with the prospect of becoming a permanent homemaker after years of professional engagement, the fear of being unnoticed and unmissed at the workplace loomed large. This anxiety fueled her determination to seek opportunities where she could fully utilize her potential, turning a personal struggle into a narrative of resilience and empowerment.

The year 2019 marked a significant shift in Kavita's life. Fueled by her own struggles, she founded the "Career After Family Enterprise (CAFE)" community, a social network designed to empower women seeking to establish their identities beyond the roles of wife and mother. This endeavor arose from a deep understanding of the challenges faced by women who, like her, felt their potential was constrained within the walls of tradition.

In Kavita's current years, she finds unparalleled happiness in contributing to the betterment of other women's lives. Her journey from a career-driven woman grappling with societal expectations to a catalyst for change reflects the transformative power of embracing one's true calling.

In the broader context of Kavita's journey, the story delves into the importance of women empowerment and fair practices which emerge as a guiding principle that shapes not only her professional endeavors but also the ethos of the Career After Family Enterprise (CAFE) community. Kavita firmly believes that true empowerment extends beyond personal success; it necessitates creating a landscape where fairness and integrity thrive. Ethical practices, in her perspective, are the bedrock of sustainable and meaningful progress. Within CAFE, Kavita fosters an environment where transparency, fair decision-making, and respect form the cornerstone of interactions. Recognizing that genuine empowerment is incomplete without fairness in professional engagements, she advocates for a paradigm shift where success is not measured merely by financial gains but by the positive impact on individuals and the community as a whole. Kavita's commitment to fair practices is a testament to her belief that true empowerment stems from a harmonious blend of personal growth and collective well-being, ensuring that the path to success is built on principles that stand the test of time.

As Kavita delved into the nuances of her journey, the desire to empower other women became a driving force. The founding of Career After Family Enterprise (CAFE) was not merely a professional endeavor but a heartfelt commitment to provide a platform for women to reclaim their identities. In her own struggle to balance career aspirations with societal expectations, Kavita recognized the universality of this challenge. CAFE became a sanctuary where women could share their stories, triumphs, and tribulations—a space for collective growth and empowerment.

Kavita's story is not just about her individual triumphs; it's a testament to the strength that arises when women are given the space to flourish. Her commitment is reflected in CAFE's ethos, where mutual respect, collaboration, and the celebration of diverse talents are foundational principles. Her journey resonates as a powerful ode to the indomitable spirit of women breaking barriers, rewriting their stories, and creating spaces for others to do the same.

In shadows cast by doubts and fears,
A woman rises, dispelling tears.
With strength untold, a beacon bright,
She empowers others to take flight.
Her words are seeds in fertile ground,
Empowering echoes all around.
A mentor's touch, a guiding hand,
She helps others to understand.
In unity's embrace, a sisterhood strong,
She nurtures dreams, where they belong.
Through challenges faced and battles won,
She shows the power of getting things done.
With grace that flows in rivers wide,
She breaks the chains, side by side.
A force of change, a resilient queen,
In every woman, her spirit is seen.
Through storms of life and trials faced,

She stands undaunted, beautifully graced.
An inspiration to the hearts she's known,
A woman empowering, seeds of courage sown.

15

Inspiring Confidence in Others

Shashi Jain

"The strongest action for a woman is to love herself, be herself and shine amongst those who never believed she could"

She has always been a people's person who loved interacting and knowing about them. Her friends found it easy to share their life stories with her. She also had a deep sense and love for elegant dressing and a poised demeanor from a very young age. She would often tell her parents and sisters the best way to dress that suited their skin color, personality and body shape.

This bubbly, exuberant and highly positive young girl had such a beautiful persona that was soon going to help people transform their personalities in the most wonderful way. Full of energy and enthusiasm, she was set to tell the world that a person's image is about knowing oneself and finding your self-worth, it is about self-expression & sending across the right messages through your image to others in all walks of life.

Born in Forbesganj, Bihar and brought up in a secured environment in Kolkata, Shashi had the love and care of her parents, along with the joyful company of her four sisters. Her parents always imbibed in them high values like kindness, empathy, sacrifice, respect, love, non-violence and were taught to live a disciplined, healthy and content life. Brought up in the midst of other kids, they all learnt the virtues of sharing and caring from the very beginning. Always a bright student, Shashi completed her schooling from Ballygunge Shiksha Sadan and topped in the Madhyamik examination in her school. She completed her graduation from Sivanath Shastri College and along with academics carried a great interest in classical dance and music too. She has been highly influenced by her father throughout life and he has remained her biggest support and backbone always. A great human being and beautiful soul, he taught her and all the other children strong moral values such as patience, sacrifice, respect, love and above all service to mankind. Due to his selfless service towards the society, while working with various leading NGO'S and organizations to work for the betterment and upliftment of different strata of the community, Shashi has picked up all these traits from him and is on a mission to empower people around her, especially women.

Shashi got married at the age of 23 and adjusted herself according to her husband's and family's needs. A doting wife, dutiful daughter in law, she forgot about her dreams and aspirations as her life revolved around her family completely. She was soon blessed with a lovely daughter and even though she thoroughly enjoyed her new role, responsibilities increased multifold, leaving no time for her to think about a career. But the forever positive and exuberant Shashi did not brood ever and carried on with life, ignoring the problems she faced daily. But as they say, life has other plans and when she thought everything was okay, problems in her married life increased and rose to such a level that she had to take the drastic step of moving out of her 15 year long marriage. This decision to separate was the most difficult for her considering the emotional person she is. Moreover, she did not possess any degree or qualification to manage her life, earn a living, be financially independent and bring up her daughter. The thought of not being able to give her daughter a normal family life was extremely heart wrenching for her as well. The struggles and hardships she faced when she started her journey alone were tremendous, along with the depression she was trying so hard to battle. She faced various financial challenges along with a fear of being judged, ridiculed, criticized by the society and many more. Shashi was afraid of the social stigma regarding separation and therefore lacked self confidence and had the fear of failing over and over again. But, she also knew that she had to bounce back and she slowly started rebuilding herself, brick by brick.

Shashi pursued the course in Image Consultancy & Soft Skills training and kickstarted her training career at the age of 42, an age when women are usually seen enjoying personal happiness and financial stability. Her main challenge was to compete and stand against stalwarts who had already made their mark in the field. As for her, she had no exposure to worldly affairs, no network, no database, had never managed her finances but she decided to take it all head on and besides the confidence she had in herself, she got immense support from her family who encouraged and applauded her at every step. Shashi resumed studies at the age of 45 to upgrade her knowledge in General Insurance and due to sheer grit and determination, she successfully completed the certification of Associateship in the year 2021, after a long gap of 23 years. She had self doubts when she restarted but the qualification boosted her self worth and self confidence, reinforcing the thought that, 'If you believe it, you can achieve'. Shashi has never looked back ever since then and likes calling herself, 'A constant work in progress'. She is continuing her academic journey and is currently pursuing "Fellowship" from Insurance Institute of India. She never considered her age to be a barrier or an obstacle to follow her dreams and pursue all the goals she had set for herself. She worked hard, never gave up and kept striving consistently on the path that has eventually lead her towards her passion and vision.

An image consultant, soft skills trainer and life coach by profession, Shashi Jain has adopted a conscious approach to holistic development of an individual and has thus helped people identify their self image and use clothes, apparel, appropriate body language, etiquette and verbal and vocal communication as a resource and work on the psyche and mindset that in turn helps them to improve their self worth, self confidence, capability and credibility. Shashi took a leap in life when she could no longer see her self worth and self esteem being crushed regularly. She took the leap to stand for her point of view, rights, beliefs and be fearless and assertive. After finding her own identity she now empowers other women through her training/coaching and is actively associated with many women organizations & NGOs. She was recently awarded as a "CHANGEMAKER" at a prestigious platform and is currently the chief Secretary of JITO Ladies Wing Kolkata, an organization of around 800 women where their mission is upskilling, enhancement of knowledge & empowering women in all spheres.

Along with her daughter who has now grown into a fine young woman carving her niche in the professional world, Shashi advices women to be financially independent as even if life throws several challenges and catches them unawares, they should be prepared well enough to sail through the stormy seas. One should be able to run their life smoothly therefore keep upskilling yourself and never stop learning. Never ever compromise on your self-respect at any cost as your respect is negotiable. Women like Shashi Jain are an inspiration for those who are fighting their own demons and several other battles everyday. Hardships on one side, Shashi managed to show the true potential of a woman and has become a hero by giving a new life to herself and her daughter. Besides all the struggles she went through, she still has her values undefeated. Her story may give you a silver lining and leave you with a bittersweet feeling but one thing is for sure that her story will motivate you and restore your faith.

In the world of elegance, where confidence blooms,
An image consultant crafts in mirrored rooms.
With an artist's eye and a stylist's flair,
They weave transformations, an aesthetic affair.
Colors and textures, a palette refined,
They sculpt first impressions, a visual bind.
In the mirror's reflection, a journey unfolds,
An image consultant, their story told.
From wardrobe whispers to the sway of a gait,
They refine each detail, harmonizing the state.
Confidence tailored, like a bespoke attire,
In the art of self-image, they inspire.
A smile that radiates, a posture so poised,
An image consultant, where beauty's rejoiced.
In the nuances of presentation, a delicate dance,
They choreograph elegance, giving life a chance.
In the mirror's embrace, self-assurance gleams,
As an image consultant unveils dreams.
Through the prism of style, confidence refined,
A poetic transformation, in every design.
In the tapestry of self, a consultant's touch,
An artist sculpting confidence, layer by clutch.
With every suggestion, a metamorphosis seen,
An image consultant, where beauty convenes.

16

From Kolkata's Hues to ELEGANCE

Sharda Kasera

"In the alchemy of design, she shapes dreams into wearable poetry, each piece a reflection of passion forged in precious metals—a testament to the eternal dance between craftsmanship and beauty"

During her young days, nestled in the vibrant city of Kolkata, she harbored aspirations that reached beyond the conventional roles, society often dictated for women. While others might have envisioned a more traditional path, her dreams were laced with the entrepreneurial spirit. Even in her youth, she exhibited a keen sense of independence and a desire to create something uniquely her own. The bustling markets and diverse culture of Kolkata fueled her imagination, planting the seeds of entrepreneurship in her fertile mind. Little did she know that these early inklings of ambition would later blossom into a full-fledged entrepreneurial journey, proving that the seeds of passion sown in youth can endure the test of time and eventually flourish into a remarkable and fulfilling reality.

In the heart of the bustling city, Sharda Kasera, a woman of timeless grace, sits surrounded by the sparkling fruits of her creativity in a well-lit office. Her journey from the quiet lanes of Kolkata to the vibrant tapestry of Kathmandu, where life took an unexpected turn, weaves a story of resilience and the unwavering pursuit of dreams.

Sharda's childhood was a canvas painted with the hues of familial warmth and encouragement. Growing up with loving siblings and parents who fostered a spirit of exploration, she imbibed a myriad of skills and developed a versatile personality. Little did she know that these formative years would lay the groundwork for a remarkable entrepreneurial venture later in life.

Life unfolded, and Sharda dedicated years to nurturing her family, a role she cherished. However, destiny had more chapters to add to her story. As her children embarked on their own journeys, Sharda found herself at a juncture that many might view as the winding down of life's adventures. Yet, for her, it was a crossroads, an opportunity to redefine her purpose.

The catalyst for change came when faced with the solitude that followed her daughter's marriage and her son's move to the United States. Rather than succumbing to the echoes of an empty nest, Sharda embraced the newfound freedom. Her decision to enroll in a Gems and Jewelry course marked the beginning of a transformative journey.

The turning point came when the challenge of loneliness morphed into an opportunity for self-discovery. Sharda's love for jewelry, kindled in her early years, became the guiding light. The creation of her own brand, 'ELEGANCE,' wasn't just a business venture; it was a testament to her resilience and a celebration of her journey of self-discovery and entrepreneurship.

Even though her business venture did not taste success overnight, it taught her several lessons. Sharda's advice, "Do what you can, with what you have, where you are," echoes the wisdom of her experiences. It's a rallying cry for those who hesitate to embark on their own journeys, a reminder that dreams are not bound by age or circumstance. Sharda's story serves as an anthem for breaking free from societal expectations and embracing the transformative power of pursuing one's passions.

In her entrepreneurial pursuits, Sharda Kasera doesn't just craft exquisite jewelry; she weaves ethics into every piece. 'ELEGANCE' stands not only for beauty but for ethical craftsmanship. Sharda's commitment to fair business practices underscores her belief that success should contribute positively to the community and the industry.

Sharda's tale is a beacon of inspiration for women across generations. Her late-blooming success exemplifies that it's never too late to pursue dreams. With each chapter of her story, Sharda encourages women to embrace change, challenge societal expectations, and redefine their narratives. Her journey becomes a roadmap for every woman seeking the courage to take that plunge into the unknown and carve a path uniquely her own.

Sharda Kasera's jewelry designs are an embodiment of her rich life experiences and creative spirit. Each piece tells a story, a fusion of traditional craftsmanship with a contemporary twist, echoing the diverse influences that have shaped Sharda's journey. The delicate intricacies of her designs are a testament to the meticulous attention she devotes to each creation, resulting in jewelry that not only adorns but also narrates a narrative of passion and perseverance.

'ELEGANCE,' Sharda's eponymous brand, is a showcase of her exquisite craftsmanship. Her commitment to quality and detail is evident in every facet of her creations. Whether it's a carefully sculpted necklace, a pair of ornate earrings, or a bespoke ring, each piece reflects the artistry and dedication that define Sharda's work.

Sharda takes inspiration from her cultural roots, infusing her designs with elements that pay homage to her heritage. The use of locally sourced gemstones and metals not only adds authenticity to her pieces but also contributes to sustainable and responsible practices within the jewelry industry.

What sets Sharda apart is her ability to blend tradition with innovation. Her designs seamlessly bridge the gap between timeless elegance and contemporary flair, catering to a diverse clientele with varied tastes. The jewelry emanates a timeless charm, making it suitable for both special occasions and everyday wear, a testament to Sharda's versatility as a designer.

Customers are drawn not only to the aesthetic appeal of Sharda's creations but also to the stories embedded within them. Each piece carries a part of Sharda's journey, creating a connection between the wearer and the artisan. It's this personal touch that transforms 'ELEGANCE' into more than a brand; it becomes a reflection of the artistry and resilience embodied by Sharda Kasera herself.

'ELEGANCE' not only offers stunning jewelry but also operates with a consciousness that aligns with contemporary values. This ethical approach adds an extra layer of beauty to every piece, making it not just an accessory but a statement of responsible luxury.

In the world of Sharda Kasera, each piece is a masterpiece, a harmonious blend of tradition and innovation, craftsmanship and conscience. Through her jewelry designs, Sharda continues to inspire, leaving an indelible mark on the industry and showcasing the transformative power of passion, creativity, and unwavering dedication.

In the quiet studio, gems aglow,
A jewelry designer's talents show.
Crafting tales in silver and gold,
Each creation, a story to be told.
With nimble hands and an artist's eye,

In precious metals, dreams do fly.
In every bead and delicate chain,
An artisan's passion leaves its stain.
Gemstones whisper secrets rare,
In the hands of one who truly cares.
Designs unfold, like petals bloom,
A jewelry designer, weaving a loom.
From graceful necklaces to rings so fine,
An alchemist of beauty, in every design.
In each crafted piece, a narrative spun,
A jeweler's art, radiant under the sun.

17

Coloring Innermost Cores

Madhuri Mantri

"Brushstrokes of imagination on the canvas of creativity, a painter unveils a world where colors speak louder than words"

She sat looking at the city outside. Everyone seemed to be running - some for work, some to fulfil their dream. The extreme energy and fast-paced life of the people she saw from her balcony was deeply etched in her mind and would remain the same forever. From the everlasting beauty of the city during monsoon's, the clear skyline with clouds as visible as possible, raindrops embracing her face like a gentle breeze, a cup of warm chai in her tender hands, she was soaking it all within her innocent heart. The gorgeous colours of the rainbow that peeped out of the clouds after the rain, mesmerized her and filled her mind with beautiful colours. She knew back then that she would remain a SOBO girl all her life.

Lines, circles and patterns when splattered with colors create magnificent pieces of art. The value of the art lies in the fact that it takes the meaning that its viewer wants. Every art piece speaks in a different language every time and every artist understands the language the viewer would want to hear and see, and therefore tries her best to deliver the same. Art in any form - no matter whether you choose to create it or simply observe and enjoy it - is a relaxing and inspiring activity for many people. There are innumerable people across the globe who have pursued art as a hobby, passion or profession but then there are some who tend to get lost in the flow of the patterns and colors and create masterpieces.

Born and brought up in Mumbai, Madhuri Mantri is the younger of two children. Being the youngest in the family, she always knew how to get her way around things. Her family initially lived in Andheri but later shifted to South Mumbai where she spent the best days of her life. Her father is a self-made man who rose from humble beginnings and along with her mother gave a strong set of values to both the children. From early childhood, Madhuri and her elder brother were taught the value of time, money, family ties and the art of adjustments. These strong values helped Madhuri to have her feet set firmly on the ground even when she was enjoying luxurious vacations, shopping sprees etc. She got married at the age of 21 and feels lucky to have two set of parents as the ceremony of kanyadaan was performed by her brother and bhabhi as well.

Along with her father, Madhuri's mother has always been a pillar of strength, motivation and encouragement in all that she has done. From teaching her to stay calm, value relationships and pursuing her hobby as a profession, her mom has been her go to person throughout. Along with an extremely loving family before marriage, Madhuri feels blessed to have a spouse who understands and supports her at every step. She feels glad and fortunate to have spent the happiest days of her life with her husband and two beautiful children.

A textile designer by education, Madhuri was a quintessential homemaker after marriage. She was always interested in art and painting and decided to pursue the same as a hobby in the year 2016 when she started learning canvas painting. Seeing her passion, dedication and beauty of the art pieces she created, her friends and family gave her a few orders but the real break came during the pandemic. When the whole world was trying hard to cope up with the unprecedented lockdown, Madhuri learnt and practised Mandala art forms, which played the role of meditation during the turbulent period. She decided to open an Instagram account to merely showcase her hobby but her followers kept increasing slowly, and gradually her hobby turned into a profession. Madhuri is currently specializing in Mandala art forms on various decorative pieces for home décor. She had also started taking mandala art classes for children during their vacations, which has become a regular feature now.

Life has not always been hunky-dory for Madhuri as she has faced quite a few ups and downs in her life. In the year 2003, she gave birth to her son and was experiencing one of the most happiest times but during the end of the year, her mother-in-law, father and husband had to be hospitalised due to various critical ailments. They all recovered subsequently but this period proved to be quite draining for Madhuri, both physically and emotionally. She was also very active in Ladies Circle at one point of time but slowly withdrew herself from there as retirement got closer. From being extremely busy to not doing anything affected her quite a bit, as this made her feel lost and negligible. She indulged in painting and tried her best to keep herself busy but what began as a hobby and a creative outlet has now grown into a small business.

Madhuri is exceedingly proud of the fact that the work she does is a one-woman show where she handles everything from taking orders, getting approvals from clients, sourcing raw material, executing the order, taking pictures and videos for her social media handles and finally packing and delivering. Her passion for learning new things had made her excel in everything she has done so far. Madhuri feels that the world would not have been devoid of her creativity had she pursued her passion much before she actually did, therefore she strongly believes that every woman should have faith in her own capabilities. When you believe in yourself you can overcome self doubt and have the confidence to take action and get things done. Discover what you are really good at, and work at becoming greater. Because until you spread your wings, you will have no idea how far you can fly.

In the sanctum of creation, where muses play,
An artist's spirit, a beacon in the day.
With a palette of dreams, colors aglow,
They paint stories, letting imaginations grow.
With every brushstroke, a dance of grace,
An artist conjures worlds in an intimate space.
From swirling landscapes to portraits profound,
They breathe life into canvases, visions unbound.
In the studio's hush, where inspiration is spun,
An artist's journey has only begun.
With sketches that echo the soul's gentle hum,
They capture emotions, where feelings become.
From the stroke of midnight to the dawn's first light,
An artist translates shadows into sheer delight.
In the symphony of colors, emotions unfold,
A canvas whispers stories, both young and old.
With hands that sculpt clay or craft with finesse,
An artist's hands shape visions, nothing less.
In the silence where creativity sparks,
They illuminate the world with passion's arcs.
Through galleries adorned with dreams set free,
An artist's legacy, an odyssey.
A storyteller with colors, a visionary's flight,
They paint existence with the hues of light.

18

Bold Beginnings

Sarla Newatia

"In the tapestry of life, bold beginnings weave a story of resilience and triumph—a testament to the strength found within, where courage unfolds and fearlessness prevails"

As a young girl, she embodied fearlessness and boldness, traits instilled in her by her father. Growing up, her childhood was a tapestry woven with laughter and joy. Her father's influence shaped her into a lionhearted spirit, teaching her not only to face challenges head-on but to embrace life with courage. She navigated the world with a determination that hinted at the remarkable journey awaiting her—a journey that would see her transform challenges into triumphs, embodying the very essence of resilience and boldness that defined her youth.

Born in Burma (Myanmar) and brought up in Nepal, Sarla Newatia fondly reflects on a childhood brimming with joy, surrounded by the laughter and camaraderie of four sisters and two brothers. The foundation of her character was shaped by the strong influence of her father, a respected clothes merchant, who instilled in her the virtues of bravery and boldness. Her mother, a figure of boundless love, added warmth to her formative years, creating a nurturing environment that would later become the anchor of Sarla's resilience. Growing up in a close-knit family, Sarla imbibed values that would guide her through the challenges and triumphs of life. The vivid memories of her carefree youth in Burma serve as a poignant backdrop to the woman she has become – a testament to the strength derived from familial bonds and early life lessons.

In the tapestry of Sarla Newatia's life, the threads of joy and sorrow intricately weave together. The pivotal moment arrived with the loss of her father-in-law and husband respectively, casting a shadow over her world. Grief became a heavy cloak, yet within this darkness emerged a beacon of hope – her young son, Raghav. As a widow, Sarla was confronted with the daunting task of navigating life's challenges alone. The dual roles of a grieving wife and a new entrepreneur unfolded, creating a landscape where resilience became not just a choice but a necessity.

The decision to establish a girl's guest house, born out of practicality and a need to work from home, marked a significant turning point. This venture, though a lifeline for Sarla, was not without its difficulties. The delicate balance between tending to her familial duties and steering a nascent business tested her mettle. The walls of her home bear witness to the echoes of laughter, tears, and the quiet determination that propels her forward. In this chapter of her life, Sarla faced the unfamiliar terrain of entrepreneurship, grappling with the absence of her life partner and the stark reality of shouldering responsibilities single-handedly. Yet, fueled by an indomitable spirit and driven by love for her son, she embarked on a journey where each challenge became a stepping stone towards a brighter future.

In the aftermath of her husband's departure, Sarla Newatia found herself standing at a crossroads, uncertain about the path ahead. The void left by the loss of her life partner, coupled with the simultaneous departure of her father-in-law, cast a profound shadow over her existence. It was during those trying times that the true measure of Sarla's character came to the forefront. Faced with the daunting prospect of charting her course as a widow and a new entrepreneur, she confronted the harsh reality of not only personal grief but also the practical challenges of sustaining a livelihood. The guest house, though a sanctuary for many, became a symbol of Sarla's resilience and adaptability.

The intricacies of managing a household, attending to family members, and steering a budding business unfolded as a complex tapestry. Sarla's determination became the guiding force, transforming her challenges into opportunities for growth. The learning curve of entrepreneurship, coupled with the emotional weight of loss, propeled her into uncharted territory. Yet, buoyed by the unwavering support of her son Raghav, Sarla emerged not only as a survivor but as a testament to the strength that lies within the human spirit.

Her story is not just one of overcoming adversity but a narrative of forging ahead with grace and fortitude. Sarla Newatia's journey as a widow and an entrepreneur becomes a testament to the resilience of the human spirit, showcasing that even in the face of profound loss, new beginnings can unfold with determination, hard work, and an unyielding belief in one's abilities.

Amidst the trials and tribulations of her journey, Sarla Newatia discovered that her mantra for navigating life's challenges is rooted in hard work and sheer determination. The resilience that defines her character is not merely a response to adversity; it became a conscious choice to embrace life's complexities with an indomitable spirit.

The aftermath of her husband's death left Sarla unsure of the path ahead. Yet, propelled by a vision of a better future for herself and her son, she channeled her grief into a source of strength. Her journey mirrors a phoenix rising from the ashes, turning pain into purpose and loss into a catalyst for personal growth.

As a widow and an entrepreneur, Sarla reshaped her identity, defying societal expectations and stereotypes. The challenges of managing a business single-handedly, coupled with the emotional weight of personal loss, molded her into a woman who not only survives but thrives. Through hard work, determination, and an unyielding belief in her capabilities, Sarla Newatia transformed adversity into an opportunity to redefine her life.

In the corridors of her guest house, where the echoes of laughter and shared stories reverberate, Sarla's story unfolds as a testament to the resilience innate in every individual. Her journey stands as a beacon of inspiration, illustrating that even in the face of profound difficulty, one can sculpt a meaningful and successful life through perseverance, fortitude, and an unshakeable belief in one's own strength. Her life, marked by both loss and triumph, becomes a living testament to the human capacity for resilience and the power of a determined spirit.

Sarla Newatia's commitment to running her business with fairness and honesty echoes the core values that define her journey. The girl's guest house she owns becomes more than a mere accommodation; it transforms into a haven where guests experience a genuine sense of being welcomed into a "home away from home." Sarla's dedication to providing this comforting atmosphere reflects not only in the physical spaces she manages but also in the ethos she cultivates.

The challenges of life have not made Sarla cynical or deterred her from maintaining a strong moral compass. She understands the profound impact of her role, not just as a business owner but as a provider of solace for her guests. In her pursuit of success, she prioritizes integrity, ensuring that her guests are not just customers but individuals who find warmth, security, and a sense of belonging under her roof.

Sarla's belief in the strength and power inherent in every woman is not just a personal philosophy but a guiding principle in how she conducts her business. By embodying resilience and determination, she not only achieves success on her terms but also becomes an inspiring figure for others. Through her actions, Sarla sends a powerful message that challenges and adversities can be overcome with self-belief and hard work.

Her story becomes a narrative not just of personal triumph but also of the broader empowerment of women. Her journey emphasizes that regardless of societal expectations or personal tragedies, women have the capability to shape their destinies. In running her business with authenticity and compassion, she stands as a beacon, illustrating that success is not solely measured in financial gains but in the positive impact one has on the lives of others.

In the echo of her laughter-filled childhood in Burma to the bustling corridors of her girl's guest house, Sarla's life comes full circle. Her story exemplifies that with resilience, determination, and an unwavering spirit, one can shape a life that aligns with one's dreams and aspirations. Sarla Newatia's journey stands as a testament to the enduring human capacity to overcome challenges and create a life that is not only successful but also deeply meaningful.

> ***In Burma's embrace, a spirit bold,***
> ***Young Sarla's tale, yet to be told.***
> ***With lion's heart, she faced the day,***
> ***In laughter's echo, she found her way.***
> ***Loss and grief, a tempest's might,***
> ***Yet courage fueled her fearless flight.***

Entrepreneur's path, a winding road,
In each challenge, resilience glowed.
A girl's guest house, a haven true,
Where echoes of joy and sorrow drew.
Triumphs born from shadows deep,
In Sarla's journey, promises to keep.
Fearless threads, resilience spun,
In the rising dawn and setting sun.
A tale of strength, a journey's art,
Sarla's bold beginning, a beating heart.

19

Lead, Inspire, Transform

Prerna Kothari Fomra

"A bird sitting on a tree is never afraid of the branch breaking, because it's trust is not on the branch but on it's own wings. Always believe in yourself"

The living room brimmed with incessant chatter once the elders were back from work and the young ones were back from school. Evenings were a time for reunion where all 13 members of the family lived together under one roof and shared values and harmonious coexistence. There was so much love and joy around that there was absolutely no time for anyone to get bored. No doubt, being the youngest girl child of her family she was over-pampered but she had her priorities set from the very beginning. A house with so many members was indeed a place of great hustle and bustle which was normal for this petite girl. Most of the year was celebratory with birthdays, anniversaries, weddings and family gatherings. She never really felt the need to make too many friends and as for boredom…well that word did not exist in her dictionary. This pretty, dainty girl was set to accomplish greater things in life and mingle with those with whom normal people crave to get close to.

Don't we all know that a girl should be two things – who and what she wants? Women these days take these words very seriously as they break the societal norms and hop on the journey they want to explore. The world often expects women to stay home, take care of the family, get married and give birth to children. However, women these days differ from this thought and even if they give their families utmost priority, careers and professions are also given topmost preference.

Born in the City of Joy Kolkata, Prerna Kothari Fomra enjoyed growing up in a joint family and the same happiness she experienced when she got married too. Highly influenced by many members of her family, Prerna feels grateful to have imbibed the best of values and character traits from not one but many. Her mother always believed in her and taught her to be honest and trustworthy. She gave Prerna full liberty to do whatever she wanted to but at the same time explained to her the importance of remaining transparent in all her relationships – whether professional or personal. Her father is an inspiration for her because of his strong ethics, hard work and excellent organizational skills and has taught her some amazing networking and social skills. Her parents have always been more as friends and that's one of the reasons behind the strength in Prerna's nature. Apart from her parents, she also shares a very strong and special bond with her elder sister who is more like a role model for her. Being elder to her by 6 years, her sister has always protected her and doted on her like a second mother. Her aunt and uncle have also played a quintessential part in helping shape her life.

As a student, Prerna was average in class and disliked Mathematics as a subject and could manage to barely pass and therefore she decided to opt for humanities in Class 11. She developed deep interest in the course she was pursuing and managed to rank 1st or 2nd in college. This gave an amazing boost and confidence to her personality. Another instance that added on to her confidence was when she went for a short course to Shobha Indani Institute of cultural classes Pune and won the title of SICC Miss World. This further made her believe in her capabilities and helped her stand out in the crowd.

Prerna was never someone who could work in a 9 to 5 kind of setup, therefore she chose a profession that gave her flexibility and did not require her to stay away from her family. She runs her own company called Media Connect that is into PR, events, bollywood movie promotions, celebrity management, media relations, organizing press conferences, newspaper coverages, advertisements and marketing. The industry she has chosen has given her vast opportunities to network and work with clients from all walks of life. Prerna believes that everyday is a new learning experience and is never boring because of continuous interactions with people from the glamorous world.

Prerna feels blessed to have been married to a man who completely understands her. Her husband Raghav has always been very supportive and respected her work along with giving her full freedom to work independently. He always pushes her from behind and helps her regain her balance whenever she is about to fall. Her business partner Ankit and his family have also been one of the biggest reasons behind her success. She and Ankit make a solid team and have worked together to build a wonderful team that is doing some amazing work.

Often when faced with failure or adversities, we are tempted to stop. It's not easy to bounce back wholeheartedly from any misstep in your endeavors, whether be it in a business venture, in your personal life or in any other aspect. But those with courage to get back up, learn from their mistakes and give it another go, are the ones who truly have a chance towards success. Prerna Kothari Fomra is one such brilliant woman who has had to overcome failures and obstacles before seeing the impressive achievements she has today. She strongly believes that God has given supreme powers to women which give them the ability to balance all aspects of their lives, be it work, family, children, household, parents, helpers, career, studies, social life etc. As a woman and a mother, Prerna has had to balance and maintain a tight rope walk between her home and her career. She is truly an inspiration and a role model to all women who aspire to dream and achieve big.

In the realm of ventures, where dreams take flight,
An inspiring entrepreneur, a beacon of light.
With a vision as vast as the open sky,
She paints success in hues that defy.
From dawn's first blush to the quiet of night,
She orchestrates businesses, her spirit alight.
In challenges faced and battles won,
Her journey, a testament to what can be done.
With every setback, resilience she weaves,
A tapestry of triumph, a woman who believes.
In boardroom battles and ventures anew,
She blazes trails, breaking through.
Her hands craft empires from dreams once small,
A symphony of resilience, heard by all.
Through every hurdle, every test,
She builds a legacy, a tale of zest.
In a world where glass ceilings break,
She paves the way, an entrepreneur's wake.
A leader who empowers, inspires the next,
Her footsteps echo, leaving a lasting text.
With courage as her compass, determination her guide,
An inspiring woman entrepreneur, in every stride.
In the entrepreneurial landscape, her story's spun,
A saga of resilience, of battles won.

20

Feast of Ambition

Vanita Bajoria

"Her culinary empire is a testament to the fusion of vision and flavor, where each restaurant is a chapter in the gastronomic tale written by a woman with a palate for success"

In the bustling city of Chennai, amidst the vibrant tapestry of her youth, a young girl emerged as a dreamer with aspirations that soared beyond the ordinary. From the earliest days of her childhood, she harbored a vision that transcended the boundaries of conventional expectations. The eldest of four siblings, her upbringing was marked by the warmth of a loving family, where her parents, especially her mother, played pivotal roles in fostering her dreams. As she navigated the corridors of her formative years, she found herself drawn to the world of commerce, nurturing ambitions that whispered of entrepreneurial pursuits. Her vivid imagination painted a future where she would stand as a beacon of success, a trailblazing businesswoman shaping her destiny against the backdrop of a fast-paced and competitive world. Little did she know that these early dreams would pave the way for a remarkable journey of resilience, determination, and triumph.

Born into a family of four siblings, in the bustling city of Chennai, Vanita being the eldest, experienced the warmth of being a pampered child. Her parents, particularly her mother, played a significant role in ensuring that she never missed out on the good things life had to offer.

As she traversed through childhood, the bond with her mother became the cornerstone of her life. Constant motivation and encouragement from her mother fueled her growth, creating a special connection that transcended the ordinary. Despite the inevitable challenges that every family faces, they weathered the storms together.

Fast forward to her adolescence and early adulthood, the years were filled with peer pressure and insecurities. It was a testing phase, but with her mother's unwavering support, she navigated through the turbulence. Those challenging years set the stage for her resilience and determination.

Needless to say, the most influential figure in Vanita's life emerged as her mother. The woman who not only nurtured her but instilled the values that would shape her future. Their bond became the source of strength and inspiration, paving the way for the woman she was destined to become.

Having shifted to Kolkata post-marriage in 2003, she became a part of a supportive and beautiful family. Over the course of two decades, her marriage blossomed into a happy and successful journey. Her family, especially her husband and in-laws, remained pillars of support throughout her entrepreneurial endeavors.

As a working mother, she found solace and purpose in managing her professional and personal responsibilities. Her son, currently pursuing B.Com (Hons) in college, stands as a testament to the balance she struck between her roles as a mother and an entrepreneur.

Following her passion for commerce, she took a leap of faith into the restaurant industry, with dreams of entrepreneurship. The journey commenced with the launch of Kolkata's first 7D Adventure Plex in January 2013. The success of this venture propelled her to open the first 11D Adventure Plex in February 2014, captivating audiences with immersive experiences.

The entrepreneurial spirit didn't stop there. In January 2015, she introduced the region's first Horror House, featuring an exhilarating vortex experience that attracted people of all ages. The journey continued with the arrival of the iconic Hard Rock Cafe in December 2017, showcasing rock-and-roll memorabilia, live music, and classic American platters.

In collaboration with her husband, she co-founded Amit Hospitality LLP in November 2018. This partnership led to bringing Lord of the Drinks to Kolkata in December 2019, followed by the launch of Veneto, a unique Italian dining establishment, in March 2022. The innovative Warehouse Café became their most recent venture in June 2022.

The happiest moment of her life unfolded when she successfully launched her own businesses, solidifying her position as a successful female entrepreneur. It was a dream transformed into reality, a testament to her dedication and hard work.

However, success wasn't handed to her on a silver platter. The journey was fraught with doubts and moments of uncertainty. The fierce competition in the fast-paced business world made her question her abilities. Yet, with experience gained and unwavering support from her partner and parents, she took the biggest leap forward, determined to achieve positive outcomes and inspire women in today's world.

Her positive mental outlook emerged as a crucial factor in her success. She believed that incorporating a positive attitude into one's lifestyle could lead to living the best life possible. The ability to see the good in every situation propelled her forward.

Mistakes were inevitable, and she embraced them as stepping stones to growth. Learning valuable lessons from each misstep, she evolved as an individual and a businesswoman.

Although, the decision to start her own business was the most difficult one she faced, along with fierce competition from her peers, but her patrons overwhelming response reassured her that it was a wise choice. The journey, though challenging, proved to be a fulfilling adventure.

Reflecting on the leap and her life thereafter, Vanita Bajoria acknowledges the importance of time management. Balancing her professional and personal life, especially as a working mother was a constant challenge. She says that if given a chance to start over, she would prioritize learning how to manage her time more efficiently to spend quality moments with her son.

To women awaiting the opportune moment to take the leap, she offers advice rooted in her own experiences. Following one's heart and pursuing what one loves is the key to success. Financial independence, she emphasizes, is crucial for women, irrespective of their familial or marital background.

In conclusion, her story is one of resilience, determination, and the pursuit of dreams. From a pampered child in Chennai to a successful entrepreneur in Kolkata, she embodies the spirit of overcoming challenges and embracing opportunities. Her journey is a beacon of inspiration for those aspiring to take the leap and carve their own path in the world of entrepreneurship.

In the bustling rhythm of the city's heartbeat,
A woman of strength, her strides are fleet.
Entrepreneur extraordinaire, a vision in her gaze,
She builds empires where success plays.
From dawn's first light to the quiet of night,

She orchestrates kitchens, a visionary's flight.
With flavors diverse, a menu unfolds,
A story of triumph, of tales yet untold.
Tables adorned with laughter and cheer,
Her restaurants echo, drawing hearts near.
A businesswoman's grace, resilience profound,
In every success, her victories resound.
She turns challenges to stepping stones,
A leader unyielding, through unknown zones.
In the hustle of kitchens, dreams take flight,
An entrepreneur's realm, a beacon of light.
Success in recipes, in customer smiles,
A journey that spans countless miles.
In the empire she's built, a legacy spun,
A woman entrepreneur, her story begun.

21

Lights, Camera, Action

Saroj Tivary

"In the grand symphony of life, age is but a note, and the melody we create is defined by the passion, experiences, and zest we infuse into every moment"

A young girls childhood in Kolkata was marked by vivid dreams and a resilient spirit. Even at an immature age, she would often find herself lost in reveries, envisioning a future where she could create a name for herself. Growing up with dreams as vast as the Kolkata skies, she harbored aspirations that transcended the confines of traditional expectations. Her imagination fueled her determination to carve out a unique identity, setting the stage for the remarkable journey that would unfold later in life. Little did she know that those childhood dreams would become the driving force behind her unwavering pursuit of passion, success, and a legacy that defied the limitations imposed by societal norms.

Saroj Tivary's early life unfolded in Punjab and then Kolkata, marked by the challenges of an early marriage at the age of 18 while still in her first year of college. After giving birth to two children, she faced the tragedy of becoming a widow with no professional qualifications. Abandoned by her in-laws due to financial matters, Saroj found herself grappling with suicidal tendencies. However, destiny intervened, leading her back to her parents' house.

In a resilient move to rebuild her life, Saroj enrolled in a secretarial course and began working as a secretary in the office of Mr. Prashant Tivary. Their professional collaboration blossomed into a deep connection, culminating in marriage and Prashant's unwavering support, especially in refusing to separate Saroj from her children, became a defining moment in her journey towards a renewed life and love. The blended family now comprised three children – two from her first marriage and one from the second.

Despite the challenges she faced, Saroj harbored an unfulfilled childhood dream of becoming a teacher. With determination and an unyielding work ethic, she overcame the language barrier (having studied in Hindi medium schools) and pursued her goal relentlessly.

Rising at 3 am to study, Saroj took on the role of a helper teacher at St. James' School. Unsatisfied, she embarked on a journey of academic achievement, earning her graduation and B.Ed degree through distance learning. Her perseverance finally paid off as she secured a position as a Hindi teacher at St. James' School.

However, life threw another challenge her way when she developed a severe swelling in her vocal cords, causing her to lose her voice temporarily. Undeterred, Saroj faced this health setback with resilience, undergoing a lengthy hospital stay but ultimately recovering. This phase tested her strength, but she emerged from it with an undiminished spirit.

Upon retiring from her teaching career at the age of 60, Saroj embarked on a new adventure, enrolling in theatre classes under the guidance of Ramanjit Kaur, founder of The Creative Arts Academy. Seven years of dedication to the craft not only showcased her passion for the arts but also paved the way for a significant turning point in her life. Saroj's transition from teaching to theatre marked a remarkable chapter in her journey, demonstrating her willingness to embrace new challenges and follow her passions beyond the conventional expectations of retirement. This period of her life, spanning seven years, became a transformative experience that allowed her to explore and express herself in ways she hadn't before.

Her dedication and commitment to theatre were not merely a post-retirement pastime; they became a crucial part of her identity. The challenges of mastering a new craft at an age when many might choose to settle into a quieter life showcased Saroj's indomitable spirit. The theatre provided her with a platform to rediscover herself, honing her talents and embracing a creative outlet that resonated with her deeply.

This phase of Saroj's life not only enriched her personally but also laid the foundation for an unexpected career shift. The skills she cultivated during her time in theatre eventually opened doors in the advertising and movie industry, proving that it's never too late to embark on a new professional journey. Saroj's story serves as an inspiring reminder that one can find renewed purpose and success by embracing change and pursuing passions, even in the later stages of life.

Her recent venture included a trip to Mumbai for an advertisement shoot, an experience that saw her sharing the screen with none other than the iconic Shahrukh Khan. This accomplishment not only underscores Saroj's talent but also serves as a powerful testament to the fact that age should never limit one's aspirations.

Saroj's enthusiastic approach to her work, challenges preconceived notions about the capabilities of individuals in their later years. Her zest for life and passion for her craft inspire those around her, proving that age is truly just a number when it comes to pursuing one's dreams. Her family, including her proud husband and children, have become steadfast supporters of her journey, emphasizing the importance of embracing change and seizing opportunities at any stage in life. In a beautiful twist, Saroj, who had faced limited educational opportunities, ensured her children pursued professional degrees. Saroj stands as a shining example of how a determined spirit and a passion for life can lead to continuous growth and success.

Saroj Tivary's story not only challenges the traditional narrative surrounding young widows but also serves as a beacon of inspiration for individuals seeking fulfillment and success later in life. The plight of young widows often involves unnecessary pressures, discrimination, and the arduous task of rebuilding one's life against significant odds. Saroj's journey, particularly her decision to bring up her children and find love again, reflects her courage. She not only excelled in her teaching career but also proved that a setback is not the end but an opportunity for a comeback.

As she embraced a new chapter in theatre and later transitioned into the advertising and movie industry, Saroj shattered stereotypes associated with age. Her story becomes a rallying cry for individuals, especially women, to pursue their passions irrespective of limitations. At 71, Saroj has become a trailblazer, illustrating that one's passion can lead to continuous personal and professional growth. Her legacy becomes a narrative of strength, resilience, and the boundless possibilities that can unfold when one embraces life with unwavering determination.

On the stage of dreams, a spotlight gleams,
An actor, weaving vibrant scenes.
With grace that dances, and emotions untold,
Her craft unfolds, a story to behold.
In each role embraced, a chameleon's art,
She breathes life into characters, a work of heart.
From the script's ink to the stage's glow,
She brings tales to life, let the emotions flow.
Through laughter and tears, in every guise,

Her presence captivates, under stage lights' rise.
A thespian's journey, from script to bow,
In the limelight's glow, she takes her vow.
From silver screens to the theater's hush,
Her charisma echoes in every hushed shush.
In the canvas of roles, a palette so vast,
She paints emotions, from first to last.
A storyteller with expressions profound,
In the actor's realm, she is renowned.
A symphony of lines, each scene a song,
The versatile actor, where dreams belong.

22

Navigating Love, Leadership, and the Leap

Soma Roy

"Guiding leaders through the labyrinth of potential, she illuminates the path to greatness, transforming aspirations into a symphony of empowered teams and visionary triumphs"

During the initial days of her life, she would naturally assume the role of a leader among her friends, becoming the go-to person for advice and problem-solving. The intricate dynamics of her childhood laid the foundation for the balanced and empathetic individual she would evolve into. Surrounded by the love of her father and the adoration of her grandfather, she experienced a mosaic of emotions within her family. While her father's unwavering support became a guiding light, not every family member extended the same warmth. This early exposure to both love and challenges shaped her into a resilient and emotionally balanced person, with the ability to navigate various facets of life with grace. The neighborhood's leader during her formative years, she became a pillar of support for friends who sought solace and solutions, setting the stage for her future roles as a coach and psychotherapist.

In the lively city of Kolkata, nestled in the heart of Bhowanipore, Soma Roy, took her first breath. As the cherished first child of a Bengali family, her early years unfolded in a tapestry of love from her father, who influenced her life in more ways than one. His guidance molded her into a resilient and compassionate individual, instilling the values of strength and empathy. Little did she know that the lessons she had learnt back then would prove invaluable in her chosen path.

As the first chapter of her professional life unfolded, she found myself drawn to inspiring and uplifting others. This innate ability led her to become a Leadership Transformation Coach and Psychotherapist. While her corporate journey spanned various industries, the natural progression of her character guided her towards coaching.

The happiest and most satisfying moments of her life were marked by the beginning of her career after completing college. Despite starting as a telecaller earning a modest sum, the dream of achievement motivated her. Climbing the corporate ladder, she eventually reached the position of General Manager Sales and Marketing for a prestigious five-star hotel project in Kolkata.

However, life's journey wasn't without its challenges and soon she stepped into one of the most difficult phase when she decided to transition from a stable job to entrepreneurship. Launching a career as a Luxury Real Estate Marketing Consultant, she faced financial uncertainties and doubted whether she would thrive in the competitive market. Yet, with faith and determination, she not only survived but established a reputable name in the industry. Her never-give-up spirit became the cornerstone of her success.

When asked to reflect on the mistakes she made along the way, trusting people blindly stands out. However, she is quick to add that these lessons contributed to her personal and professional growth immensely. A Kolkatan by heart, leaving the city of joy to embark on a new chapter in Mumbai was the hardest decision of her life, as this shift meant leaving her comfort zone and venturing into unknown territory.

If given the chance to start anew, she is keen to emphasize more on education before venturing into business. Despite the challenges she has faced, her journey has been defined by resilience, risk-taking, and an unwavering commitment to personal and professional growth.

After navigating the challenging terrain of divorce, Soma found herself in the delicate dance of managing both personal and professional realms. Balancing the aftermath of a marriage dissolution with the demands of a burgeoning entrepreneurial journey required an unparalleled resilience. Yet, fueled by her unwavering determination, Soma tackled this dual challenge head-on. The experience served as a crucible, shaping her into a woman who could adeptly compartmentalize her personal emotions while excelling in her professional endeavors. Managing this delicate equilibrium became a testament to her strength, reinforcing her commitment to both personal growth and the pursuit of her entrepreneurial dreams.

Amidst the hustle of her professional endeavors, love unexpectedly found its way back into Soma's life. After the storm of divorce, a newfound partner entered the scene, offering a fresh chapter of warmth and companionship. This unexpected turn in her personal life became a source of joy and solace. Soma, ever resilient, embraced this new love with open arms, illustrating that life's journey is full of twists and turns, and the heart can find renewal even after challenging times. The harmony between her personal and professional spheres became a testament to her ability to navigate life's complexities with grace and authenticity.

To aspiring women contemplating a leap, her advice is simple—listen to your instincts, trust your desires, and be your own guiding force. In business, fairness is not a compromise, it's a clarity of intent. Being professional means respecting stakeholders across every facet of your business, fostering reciprocal respect and responsibility.

Soma's message to women contemplating the leap is a powerful testament to self-reliance and intuition. She advises, "Listen to your own instincts; they never lie, and follow what you desire to do because the only person you have with you is yourself." Soma underscores the importance of trusting one's inner compass, acknowledging that amidst the myriad opinions and external voices, one's instincts remain a steadfast guide. Her words carry a profound truth, encouraging women to embrace their desires and ambitions with conviction. Soma's advice echoes a call for self-empowerment, emphasizing that the journey begins by tuning into one's own aspirations and charting a path guided by personal passion and authenticity.

And so, Soma's story continues—a tapestry woven with experiences, challenges, and triumphs—a journey shaped by the echoes of Kolkata and the daring spirit that led her to Mumbai, a city of dreams and opportunities.

In the realm where ambitions dare to soar,
A Leadership Transformation Coach, wise and more.
Guiding minds through uncharted lands,
Crafting leaders with visionary hands.
In the crucible of growth, forging change,
Transforming limits, expanding the range.
A coach who nurtures, empowers the soul,
Fanning the flames of leadership's goal.
Through challenges faced, and trials embraced,
They navigate storms with steady grace.
Unveiling strengths, a beacon to find,
A coach, a guide, in hearts enshrined.
Wisdom's tapestry woven through every word,
A catalyst for transformation, often unheard.

In the dance of leadership, a steady guide,
A coach inspiring, in each stride.
They sculpt leaders with a vision clear,
Banishing doubt, dispelling fear.
In the alchemy of change, they stand,
A Leadership Transformation Coach, in demand.

23

Culinary Canvas

Sonal Athwani

"In the kitchen of life, every spice of passion, every dash of sacrifice, and every stir of resilience creates a unique recipe for success"

From an early age, the aromatic symphony of spices and the sizzle of pans captured her heart in the holy city of Varanasi. Her childhood, spent in the midst of bustling kitchens and the warmth of family gatherings, ignited an unwavering passion for cooking. Intrigued by the art of crafting flavors and creating culinary wonders, she found herself drawn to the kitchen, eager to experiment and master the intricacies of the culinary world. Her desire to achieve greatness in the profession took root in those formative years, as she envisioned a future where her culinary creations would be celebrated far beyond the confines of her family home. Little did she know that this early fascination would blossom into a lifelong journey, shaping her into a self-trained gourmet chef with a story as rich and diverse as the dishes she would one day master.

A passionate and self-taught gourmet chef Sonal Athwani, embarked on a culinary journey in the holy city of Varanasi, her life shaped by family ties and personal sacrifices. Born into a family where her father and uncle, two brothers, married two sisters, their lives took a turn when the family business separated.

Her father and uncle found their destiny in the quaint town of Raiganj, but the small-town charm couldn't accommodate both families, her father, driven by the desire for the education of his children, requested his brother to return. Sonal's uncle agreed, and together they established a brick kiln, setting the stage for her childhood spent under the care of her aunt and uncle.

Nigella Lawson's influence on Sonal blossomed into a lifelong passion for cooking. Despite the geographical separation from her parents, she embraced the responsibility of nurturing her younger siblings, honing her culinary skills through experimentation and a love for diverse cuisines.

Marriage made her shift to Pune and in the pivotal years spanning 1999 to 2018, Sonal encountered the most formidable challenges of her culinary odyssey. Faced with societal opposition and relentless attempts to dissuade her, she stood resilient. Commencing her venture in 2003 with humble tiffin services for students and professionals living away from home, Sonal gradually expanded her culinary footprint. The journey evolved to providing evening snacks, managing cafeterias for IT sectors and MNCs, and orchestrating daily meals for a staggering total of 950 individuals. These years of toil and triumph were akin to a culinary tapestry, woven with the threads of determination, hard work, and an unyielding commitment to her craft.

The decision to uproot her established ventures in Pune and embark on a fresh chapter in Kolkata due to her husband's work, epitomized the most challenging yet transformative period. It mirrored the complexities of raising a child and entrusting its care to someone else. Undeterred by the magnitude of the leap, Sonal ventured into Kolkata with a cloud kitchen, persistently building her culinary empire. Eventually, she realized her dream of owning a cafe, cementing her status as a successful entrepreneur. This phase encapsulates the profound truth that sometimes, in letting go of the familiar, one discovers the untapped potential within, crafting a narrative of resilience and determination.

Sonal, the culinary entrepreneur, has been a steadfast advocate for fair business practices throughout her illustrious journey. In her culinary venture, she ensures that ethical standards and integrity form the cornerstone of her operations. From the early days of providing tiffin services to managing cafeterias for large corporations, Sonal has prioritized transparency, honesty, and respect in all her dealings. She believes in fair compensation for her team, fostering a workplace where employees feel valued and appreciated. Additionally, Sonal is committed to sourcing quality ingredients responsibly, supporting local suppliers and promoting sustainability in her culinary creations. By upholding these ethical practices, she not only fosters a positive work environment but also gains the trust and loyalty of her customers, creating a culinary legacy built on integrity and excellence.

Belief in herself, coupled with a deep faith in God, propelled Sonal forward, but it was the unwavering support of her husband Rohitt and son Vedd that became the driving force behind her culinary pursuits. The years of struggle weren't just a tale of professional growth; they marked a personal metamorphosis. Sonal's son, her reason for existence, instilled in her the realization that her efforts shouldn't solely be for others but also for herself. Recognizing her own worth became a pivotal moment, breaking the pattern of succumbing to others' expectations. Mistakes of the past, where she often prioritized others' happiness over her own, were transformed into lessons on self-love and resilience. Her son, acting as a catalyst for change, motivated her to make a promise—to prioritize self-care and self-love, a commitment that would shape the trajectory of her life in profound ways. Sonal's determination to carve her path, free from external influences, became more evident than ever. Trusting her instincts and understanding that hard work and persistence were her allies, she embraced the challenge with an unwavering spirit.

As Sonal reflects on her extraordinary journey, she recognizes that her story holds a timeless lesson for aspiring entrepreneurs and dreamers alike. If given the chance to rewind time, she would rewrite the script with a newfound conviction—trusting her instincts, making decisions autonomously, and shunning the undue influence of others. This revelation speaks to the core of her wisdom: the ability to manage alone, understanding that hard work and persistence are the keys to success, and that there are no shortcuts in the pursuit of one's passion. Sonal's narrative echoes the importance of listening to one's heart, following one's dreams, and embracing the challenges that pave the way for personal and professional growth. Her story is a testament to the enduring power of determination, and it stands as a beacon of inspiration for those who dare to dream and embark on their unique journeys of self-discovery.

In the tapestry of time, a story unfolds,
A saga of courage, as life molds.
Through valleys of joy and mountains of strife,
We navigate the labyrinth, creating our life.
From birth's tender dawn to twilight's glow,
We dance with dreams, letting aspirations grow.
Challenges emerge, like storms at sea,
Yet, we chart our course, strong and free.
In the garden of moments, both bitter and sweet,
We sow seeds of hope with determined feat.
Fumbling through missteps, we find our way,
For each stumble teaches, come what may.
With each sunrise, a promise anew,
A chance to paint skies in shades of blue.
The symphony of laughter, the solace of tears,
Compose the melody of our fleeting years.
Through seasons of change, we stand tall,
A tapestry woven with threads that enthrall.
In the mosaic of life, each color we lend,
A masterpiece unfolds, unique to the end.

24

Journey of Rediscovery

Anuradha Kapoor

"In the symphony of life, embracing our passions and dreams is the melody that transforms existence into a timeless masterpiece. Let the whispers of your heart guide you, for within them lies the key to rediscovery and the courage to rewrite the narrative of your own story"

As a child growing up in the enchanting city of Agra, she was a spirited and curious soul. Her eyes sparkled with wonder as she explored the narrow lanes and vibrant markets of her hometown. Surrounded by the rich history and cultural tapestry of Agra, she developed an early fascination for stories, often losing herself in the pages of books that transported her to magical realms. Her laughter echoed through the streets as she played traditional games with neighborhood friends, her carefree spirit a testament to the joyous innocence of childhood. Observant and imaginative, she soaked in the vibrant hues of life, laying the foundation for the dreams that would later bloom in her heart. Little did she know that the wide-eyed girl, weaving dreams amidst the historical splendor of Agra, would one day embark on a remarkable journey of self-discovery and creativity in the bustling city of Kolkata.

As a child in the picturesque city of Agra, I was a blend of curiosity and vivacity. Roaming the narrow lanes that echoed with the tales of centuries gone by, my inquisitive gaze absorbed the historical richness surrounding me. Agra's enchanting markets became my playground, each corner an opportunity for exploration. My early years were marked by an insatiable curiosity about the world, a trait that found expression in my fascination for stories. The school library became my sanctuary, where I would lose myself in the enchanting narratives that transported me to far-off lands and ignited my imagination. Whether absorbed in books or engaging in traditional games with my neighborhood companions, my laughter resonated through the ancient streets, embodying the carefree joy of childhood. It was within this vibrant tapestry of Agra's cultural heritage that the seeds of my dreams were sown, laying the groundwork for the remarkable journey that awaited me in the years to come.

As I transitioned from childhood to adolescence, the tapestry of my dreams continued to evolve against the backdrop of Agra's historical grandeur. The cultural richness of my surroundings deeply influenced my perspective on life, instilling a sense of appreciation for tradition and storytelling. Growing up, I found myself drawn to the intricate details of local traditions and rituals, absorbing the vibrant colors and rhythms that shaped my early understanding of the world. These formative years, marked by the echoes of historical tales and the warmth of community, laid the groundwork for the values I would carry into adulthood. My journey from a spirited Agra childhood to the complexities of adolescence was a transformative period that unknowingly set the stage for the later chapters of my life—a life that would see me stepping beyond the familiar, embracing new horizons, and ultimately rediscovering myself in the bustling city of Kolkata.

My transition from the cultural embrace of Agra to the bustling city of Kolkata marked a pivotal chapter in her life. Marriage brought me to a new environment, where the vibrancy of Kolkata's streets and the cultural diversity posed both challenges and opportunities. Initially settling into the roles of a wife, daughter-in-law, and mother, I embraced the responsibilities with grace, molding myself to fit societal expectations. However, beneath the facade of contentment, a persistent sense of unfulfillment lingered. The realization that I had inadvertently invested my energy in pursuits that didn't align with my true desires came gradually, after 18 years of marriage. My journey of self-discovery was catalyzed by a profound question that haunted me – what if I were to pass away, and no one truly knew my essence? This poignant reflection became the catalyst for my courageous decision to break free from the constraints of conformity and embark on a quest to rediscover myself, ultimately leading to the pursuit of my long-suppressed passion for writing.

In the wake of this internal revelation, I found myself standing at a crossroads, grappling with the yearning to live a life that reflected my true self. The fear of anonymity and the realization that life was too fleeting to be spent without leaving an authentic mark motivated me to step out of my comfort zone. It was a daring leap into the unknown, fueled by the belief that there must be more to life than the roles I had played for nearly two decades. Embracing my newfound courage, I decided to dream again, recognizing that one is never too old to pursue passions and aspirations. With the constant and strong support of my husband and family, I began my journey into the world of writing, a realm where my thoughts, dreams, and observations could find a voice. My decision to follow my heart and pursue writing became a testament to the resilience of dreams, proving that it's never too late to redefine one's purpose and seek fulfillment on a path less traveled. In the process, I not only discovered my true calling but also illuminated the way for others who might be yearning for a similar awakening in their own lives.

With each stroke of the pen, I embarked on a transformative journey of self-expression and creativity. The decision to write became a cathartic release, allowing me to articulate the thoughts, dreams, and emotions that had long been suppressed. The world I created on paper was a reflection of my innermost self, a tapestry woven with the threads of my observations, wisdom, and experiences accumulated over the years. Writing became more than a mere pursuit; it evolved into a purpose, a means to give voice to the stories that had been silently brewing within me.

For women who find themselves at the crossroads, waiting to take the leap into the uncharted territories of their dreams, my journey could be a reminder that it's never too late to reclaim one's identity, pursue passions, and rewrite the script of one's life. The latent dreams, no matter how long suppressed, hold the potential to transform existence into a vibrant tapestry of purpose and fulfillment. For every wonan waiting to take the leap, I'll say trust in the whispers of your heart, summon the courage to dream anew, and let your aspirations become the guiding light that leads you to a life enriched by authenticity and self-discovery. The world awaits the stories only you can tell, and the journey begins with that daring step into the realm of your own dreams.

In the quiet sanctuary of words, where pages turn,
An author's pen, with tales to discern.
With ink that dances, a literary ballet,
They craft worlds where emotions hold sway.
From the first chapter to the story's end,
An author's journey, a creative blend.
In the tapestry of language, where stories are spun,
They birth characters, a life just begun.
With every sentence, a narrative unfolds,
An author's quill, where magic molds.
In the rhythm of paragraphs, a lyrical trance,
They capture moments, an eternal dance.
From whispered prose to the bold refrain,
An author's legacy, a timeless gain.

In the library of dreams, where books confer,
They write tales, where imagination can stir.
Through drafts and edits, a process refined,
An author's craft, where dreams are signed.
In the symphony of words, where chapters entwine,
They create literature, a gift divine.

www.ingramcontent.com/pod-product-compliance
Lightning Source LLC
LaVergne TN
LVHW061525070526
838199LV00009B/377